D0049439

THE
C.S. LEWIS
HOAX

THE C.S. LEWIS HOAX

KATHRYN LINDSKOOG

10209 SE Division Street, Portland, Oregon 97266

THE C. S. LEWIS HOAX
© 1988 by Kathryn Lindskoog
Published by Multnomah Press
Portland, Oregon 97266

Multnomah Press is a ministry of Multnomah School of the Bible,
8435 Northeast Glisan Street, Portland, Oregon 97220

Edited by Rodney L. Morris
Cover design by Bruce DeRoos
Cover and interior illustrations © 1988 by Patrick Wynne

Printed in the United States of America

Library of Congress Cataloging-in-Publication Data

Lindskoog, Kathryn Ann.
  The C. S. Lewis hoax.

  Includes bibliographies and index.
  1. Lewis, C. S. (Clive Staples), 1898-1963.
2. Lewis, C. S. (Clive Staples), 1898-1963—Authorship.
3. Literary forgeries and mystifications.   4. Authors,
English—20th century—Biography.   I. Title.
PR6023.E926Z779 1988   823'.912   88-28889
ISBN 0-88070-258-3

88 89 90 91 92 93 94 95 – 8 7 6 5 4 3 2 1

To Pauline Baynes,
C. S. Lewis's Chosen Illustrator,
Herself an Illustration of the Art of Living

It is almost always worth while to be cheated;
people's little frauds have an interest
which more than repays what they cost us.
Logan Pearsall Smith, *Afterthoughts* (1931)

CONTENTS

FOREWORD

Although this book is written in an entertaining way for a broad spectrum of readers, it springs from serious scholarship. If even half of the argued conjectures in it are correct—and I suspect that more than half of them are—there will have to be major revisions in the background of our understanding of Lewis. The major works, which came out in Lewis's lifetime, are not affected; but both the minor works afterwards and their critical presentation will have to be reconsidered. And let me add to that, though published after Lewis's death, "The Nameless Isle," "The Queen of Drum," and the letters to Greeves are all (in vastly different ways) major works, and their editing will have to be rechecked. (If I emphasize Lewis's books and not his life, that is my bias; others will find Lindskoog's biographical corrections more important.)

Can any of Lindskoog's arguments be dismissed? Perhaps some can. But their power is in their accumulative weight. I do not think, overall, they can be dismissed. Any *ad hominem* attack on Lindskoog will not eliminate her textual and historical arguments. Her points must be slowly and fully answered. If they are not answered, then readers of Lewis's works should share Lindskoog's suspicions. Scholars writing on Lewis should repeat Lindskoog's arguments until they reach a broad audience. What else can honest scholars do? And perhaps Collins in Britain and Macmillan and Harcourt Brace Jovanovich in the United States should do their own investigations? They would not, I assume, willingly publish as a Christian writer's works, contaminated materials. That would raise questions about all their religious books.

But I hope it will not come to that. John Henry Newman, when his honor was attacked by a fellow Christian, Charles Kingsley (in a writing far less charitable than Lindskoog's), replied greatly—*Apologia pro Vita Sua*. Walter Hooper need not be daunted by the comparison; any honest and full reply will be read with great attention. Books like Lindskoog's cause great pain at the time; her earlier essay, as mentioned in chapter 3, caused some splits between students of Lewis. But pain and controversy are necessary parts of scholarship upon occasion. They are worth suffering if truth emerges. What else is scholarship for?

Joe R. Christopher

Co-editor of *C. S. Lewis:*
An Annotated Checklist

Author of *C. S. Lewis,*
Twayne English Authors Series

PREFACE

C. S. Lewis (1898-1963) is undoubtedly our century's most popular and beloved Christian author. His books reportedly sell 1.5 million copies every year, and countless people claim they have been delighted, enlightened, strengthened, and enriched by his writing. Lewis spent most of his life teaching literature at the University of Oxford, then at Cambridge. His books range from literary scholarship to powerful fantasies for both adults and children, and from poetry to practical Christian teaching. Lewis had an unusual love for books, nature, and people. Like many others who had the pleasure of getting to know him a bit in person, I recall him as a marvelously warm, zestful, friendly, and comfortable man—twinkling with humor and burning with ideas.

Warren Lewis (1895-1973) is best known as the brother and close friend of C. S. Lewis. After gladly retiring from the military in 1932, he served as a living-companion and secretary to C. S. Lewis most of the time from then on. In middle age he quietly became an author in his own right, publishing in little over ten years seven extremely readable books about seventeenth-century France. He also compiled eleven volumes of Lewis family history, the collected letters of C. S. Lewis, and a twenty-three volume personal diary that spanned fifty years.

Two years after the death of Warren Lewis, in the course of my ongoing Lewis studies, I started discovering things I would have preferred never to learn about. Over ten years later, I was still stumbling onto new aspects of what appears to be a relentless hoax. In my distress, I contacted my friend Dr. Clyde S. Kilby about my growing concern.

On 11 September 1986, Dr. Kilby answered, "Why don't you write the whole thing up?" Early in October I called him in response, and he came in from his garden to talk with me. He was bright and healthy. Two weeks later he died in his sleep.

I have followed his final suggestion, learning more and more about the C.S. Lewis hoax as I went along. Unseemly as it may be, I offer this book in memory of Dr. Kilby—a good-natured man with clean hands and pure heart, great patience, true charity, deep faith, and bright hope. The world is better because he was here.

I have been warned repeatedly that if I dare to reveal my discoveries in this book I will be hounded by libel suits and otherwise punished. I hope that is not true. It is our legal right in this country to report facts (without malice) about public figures and to offer opinions and literary judgments; surely, it is sometimes a duty to do so. I feel called upon to do so while I am still able. I believe that no one else has had the wherewithal to discover the truth and set the record straight or it would have been done by now.

In 1987 and again in 1988, the secular media focused upon buffooneries of certain popularly revered Christian leaders, causing embarrassment, cynicism, or discouragement in various camps (in addition to some understandable glee). I have been advised that it is a disservice to the public to inform them that anything can be amiss also in C. S. Lewis affairs. But I believe that one of the most appropriate things that can happen in 1988, the twenty-fifth anniversary of C. S. Lewis's death, is for us to celebrate his gifts to us by laughing at a hoax that has gone on long enough.

ACKNOWLEDGMENTS

Within the pages of this book are the names of some of the people who read early drafts of the manuscript and generously responded with new information or encouragement: Joe R. Christopher, Arthur C. Clarke, Robert O. Evans, William Geiger, Douglas R. Gilbert, Roger Lancelyn Green, Dom Bede Griffiths, Walter Hearn, Madeleine L'Engle, Joan Ostling, George Sayer, and Sheldon Vanauken. Others included Frederick Buechner, Virginia Hearn, Richard Pierard, Faith Sand, Walter Wangerin, and Patrick Wynne. Each one gave me a valuable gift of some kind, and my thanks are profound.

I am also grateful to inadvertent contributors to this book. Carla Faust Jones merits recognition for first raising the question of the authenticity of *The Dark Tower*, and Stephen Schofield, editor of *In Search of C. S. Lewis*, deserves credit for revealing much information about C. S. Lewis affairs in his *Canadian C. S. Lewis Journal*. Those who produce *C.S.L.: The Bulletin of the New York C. S. Lewis Society* and *Mythlore* have also contributed little-known data. Lyle Dorsett and the staff of the Marion E. Wade Center at Wheaton College in Illinois are noted for their courteous help to all C. S. Lewis researchers working there, as is Dennis Porter at the Department of Western Manuscripts in Oxford's Bodleian Library.

Poet Ruth Pitter freely shared an afternoon of memories and poetry with me, enriching me with the glorious mind that gave C. S. Lewis joy. I also owe a debt of gratitude to the memory of Leonard and Mollie Miller, who eagerly told me their view of the Lewis brothers and hoped that I would pass it on to a wider audience.

I owe extraordinary thanks to K. L. Billingsley, who had the wit and zeal needed to make this book a reality. His enthusiasm never waned. I also thank Ruth Baldwin, Barbara Griffin, Nancy Hardesty, James Houston, John Lee, Ian McMurdo, Robert Siegel, Charlotte Tullock, Carolyn Vash, Clarence Walhout, Christopher Walters-Bugbee, and Charles Wrong; a few of them may not recall how they helped, but I know. Finally, thanks to my editor Rod Morris—who believed what I wrote. That was a gift indeed.

RE-PACKAGING C. S. LEWIS

The Kilns

"It's an industry, you see."

That was C. S. Lewis's rueful comment about serious literature less than a year before he died.[1] And now C. S. Lewis is a kind of literary industry himself. He has become an extremely valuable commodity. About seventy million of his books have sold so far. Careers and fortunes grow out of his popularity.[2] And hoaxes also.

This fact is no reflection upon C. S. Lewis or those who get excited about his writing. He was a scrupulously honest and humble man. It is not his fault that those who like to celebrate his thinking and writing are now sometimes accused of worshiping him. In 1984, British author Humphrey Carpenter sneered in *The Spectator* "that Lewis was God. This notion has always been hovering on the edge of what are referred to in Wheaton, Illinois, and points west as 'C. S. Lewis Studies.'"[3]

A few months after Carpenter's sarcastic article about some of C. S. Lewis's admirers, an event took place that might seem to confirm his prejudice: an eight-foot tall C. S. Lewis stained glass window was dedicated in St. Luke's Episcopal Church of Monrovia, California.[4] Actually, the window is one of several tributes in that church to outstanding teachers and workers in Christendom. But it is also an accurate reflection of the enthusiastic love that part of the public has for C. S. Lewis today. Whether that love is inordinate or not is a matter of opinion.

For many years, personal possessions of C. S. Lewis, such as an imposing wardrobe closet made by his grandfather, have been on display at the Lewis collection in Wheaton College. Now Lewis's actual home, the Kilns in Headington Quarry, Oxford, has been purchased by an American partnership originating in California. The old brick house was bought for $120,000 and turned into a museum and study center.[5] The nearby pond where Lewis swam, boated, and even ice-skated was purchased by the Berkshire, Buckinghamshire & Oxfordshire Naturalists' Trust. A sign at the entrance gate says "In 1980 the Reserve became a memorial to Henry Stephen and C. S. Lewis and will remain a place of sanctuary for Aslan, the hobbits and all natural wildlife on the Reserve."

Various C. S. Lewis conferences occur annually from northern Wales to the high desert in California. Washington, D. C. boasts a C. S. Lewis Institute for Summer Studies.[6] Various C. S. Lewis societies meet and publish newsletters decade after decade. The C. S. Lewis Centre for the study of Religion and Modernity was recently established in London, with a branch in Dallas, Texas. Many American colleges and seminaries offer credit courses on his writing.[7] C. S. Lewis calendars have been on the market for years from both Macmillan and the Thomas Cahill Company.

Since his death in 1963, at least twenty-five[8] more Lewis books have been added to the thirty-seven that were already published. Some of these posthumous volumes are just anthologies that collect and recollect, arrange and rearrange his previously published work; but some of them present writing never available before. Some of this was not intended for publication: five collections of personal letters; lecture notes; and childhood stories and drawings. All of the posthumous publications are carefully controlled and rationed out year by year.[9] At the same time, Lewis's old standbys keep coming out in new editions and varied formats—with new prefaces, new covers, new illustrations, new comments. And always with staggering sales.

Lewis is one of the most quotable writers who ever lived, and so it is no wonder that other writers like to use his words. The minimum charge from his two main United States publishers, Macmillan and Harcourt Brace Jovanovich, is twenty-five dollars. For example, an author paid this amount to quote the well-known opening sentence of the Narnian story *Voyage of the Dawn Treader*, "There was a boy named Eustace Clarence Scrubb, and he almost deserved it." It is a high price, but the sentence is almost worth it.

In 1980 a cloistered Carmelite nun in Flemington, New Jersey, wrote an excellent eighth chronicle of Narnia, telling what happened to Susan, and called it *The Centaur's Cavern*. It was so good that she soon found a Protestant publisher who wanted to bring it out. The altruistic plan was to make it extremely clear that this was *not* by C. S. Lewis, and to donate all profits to the work of Mother Teresa. One of Lewis's personal friends,

a well-known author, endorsed the project. Everyone
involved felt sure that Lewis would have approved. But
those in control of the literary estate turned the nun
down flat. Narnia was very private property, and no creative nuns were allowed to trespass in the name of charity.
Someone else was allowed to market a Narnia video game,
however, that sells for forty dollars.

No one has to buy permission to write about C. S.
Lewis, and so books about him freely abound.[10] Most
Lewis-watchers quit counting them long ago. There are
five biographies plus three versions of his life in pictures,
one biography for children, his wife's life, and selections
from his brother's diary. There are five books about the
Narnian chronicles alone, and many about his fiction in
general. There are several books telling what he believed
in various areas, and one that seeks to prove that he was
at heart a true Roman Catholic. There are also four
anthologies of essays about Lewis by people who knew
him.

There are two films about Lewis (there would undoubtedly be more if people could get permission to produce
them), and one film version of his fiction available, with
several others in production.[11] Recordings of Lewis's voice
are popular, and other people's readings of his work sell
briskly. BBC Radio produced a one-hour program of words
by and about Lewis. Much C. S. Lewis music and drama
has been created, but little of it has been performed
because rights are not available. Some fine productions
have been yanked off the market because of legal threats.
Professional actor and playwright Tom Key has delighted
audiences with his impersonation of Lewis in a one-man
show that the managers of Lewis affairs sometimes permit
him to present to nonprofit groups.

Ironically, Lewis was a man who cherished his privacy. Surely not many publicity-hungry writers have been so accessible and so popular in life and in death. Few are the center of so much attention from a variety of readers and writers. But in spite of the almost ludicrous amount of detail available to Lewis admirers, there is much confusion behind the scenes. There are claims, counter-claims, threats, bargains, questionable documents, and stories of missing documents. C. S. Lewis has become a kind of Howard Hughes of Christian literature.

In 1977, *Time* magazine devoted a page to C. S. Lewis and reported, "In May, Harcourt Brace Jovanovich released a fantasy, *The Dark Tower*, that Lewis never finished."[12] Now it seems that Lewis probably never started it. The most far-fetched fantasy of 1977 may have been the idea that Lewis was the author of *The Dark Tower*.[13] For the facts, read chapter 2, "Shining Some Light on the Dark Tower."

The preface to *The Dark Tower* tells about a disastrous three-day bonfire in which most of C. S. Lewis's apparently voluminous unpublished papers and manuscripts were destroyed. (Purported witnesses denied the story.) At the last moment a load of Lewis manuscripts was saved. The papers have never been made public, but they are gradually being published by their rescuer. Now it turns out that the published letter from an Oxford scientist all about the manuscript bonfire is in fact a hoax. For the details, read chapter 3, "Throwing Water on the Bonfire Story."

In 1979 a "documemory" film about the life and work of C. S. Lewis, featuring the voice of Peter Ustinov, premiered across the United States. It has been shown in schools and churches ever since, and a book based upon it has been issued by Macmillan. People who view the film assume that it is entirely accurate. But its misrepresentation of the people closest to C. S. Lewis and some other peculiarities make it a blend of fact and fancy. For that story, read chapter 4, "Seeing Through 'Through Joy and Beyond.'"

The producer of the "documemory" film also produced and marketed a special forty-dollar edition of *The Screwtape Letters* printed on vellum, bound in leather, and illustrated by a famous artist. But it was not illustrated by a famous artist, not real leather, not real vellum, and not even the real *Screwtape Letters*. This revised *Screwtape* sells widely in an inexpensive edition that readers take for the original as Lewis wrote it. Furthermore, many of Lewis's books now sport introductions not authorized by Lewis. And a long-lost short story by C. S. Lewis appears to be an attempt at re-creation by another person, not the real story. For the real story about these matters, read chapter 5, "Strange Visions and Revisions."

Lewis was much troubled at one time by a woman who claimed to be married to him and was not. Now it is claimed that when Lewis claimed to be married to a woman, he was not. As Lewis told the story, he had a secret legal wedding without intent of any real marriage; later, he had an ecclesiastical wedding without hope of any real marriage; and later he had the surprise of a real marriage after all. But according to his biographer, he didn't mean that he was really married; that was just a fiction used to pad a book. Fiction used to pad a book is exactly what some Lewis readers worry about nowadays. For more about Lewis's marriage, read chapter 6, "Will the Real Mrs. Lewis Stand Up."

C. S. Lewis's live-in secretary and literary assistant,[14] who was an old friend[15] and the assistant curate at his church,[16] had handwriting so much like Lewis's that he allegedly had permission to sign the letters he typed for C. S. Lewis.[17] Yet documents show that his handwriting did not look like Lewis's until years after Lewis's death. Furthermore, he was a new friend, not an old friend; and he never moved to England until after Lewis died. For an analysis of the handwriting puzzle, read chapter 7, "Forging a Friendship."[18]

C. S. Lewis's brother allegedly stole a valuable collection of 225 Lewis letters and sent them to America for safekeeping at Wheaton College in Illinois, a bastion of evangelical Christianity. Wheaton College refused to return them to the purportedly rightful owner in Oxford. The witness to the theft discovered with ultraviolet light that censored passages in the letters were about youthful sex perversions; he soberly published the entire set of stolen letters with the sex tidbits restored— in a large, serious-looking volume with a little homosexual joke for its title. For the facts about these letters, read chapter 8, "They Fall Together."

C. S. Lewis and his brother Warren were unusually creative children, and some of their fantasy world survived eighty years later. But informed readers of *Boxen: The Imaginary World of the Young C. S. Lewis* are apt to wonder what happened to Lewis's play *The King's Ring*, in which we are supposed to wonder what happened to the King's ring. There seem to be some mysterious omissions and additions in the published juvenilia. For a mature look at Lewis's immature creativity, read appendix 1, "Stealing the King's Ring." (This material proved so complex that I moved it out of the main body of the book for the sake of readers who don't want to wade through so much detail.)

All the high jinks going on in C. S. Lewis affairs are

ironic in light of Clyde S. Kilby's astute tribute to him
shortly after his death: "a man who had won, inside and
deep, a battle against pose, evasion, expedience, and the
ever-so-little lie and who wished with all his heart to
honor truth in every idea passing through his mind."[19]

Besides his commitment to truth, Lewis had also a
saving sense of humor. He might laugh at the foolishness
of the lumbering C. S. Lewis industry today and encour-
age us to do the same.

Chapter 1, Notes
 1. A conversation recorded on 4 December 1962 and published as "Unreal
    Estates" in *Of Other Worlds* by C. S. Lewis (London: Bles, 1966), 93.
 2. The following analysis of Lewis's popularity was expressed in a distin-
    guished-alumnus interview article by Wallace Kaufman titled "A Dead
    Man's Secretary" in the Summer 1987 issue of *Carolina Alumni Review*,
    28-32. (This quarterly publication of the Alumni Association of the Uni-
    versity of North Carolina at Chapel Hill boasts a circulation of forty-four
    thousand.)

    "Most probably C. S. Lewis's success is a combination of subject, quality,
    and the fact that few other writers have had a personal secretary as dedi-
    cated and selfless as Walter Hooper. . . . The series of events that brought
    Hooper and Lewis together are unlikely enough in themselves to argue a
    case of divine intervention."
 3. Humphrey Carpenter, "Giddy with Awe," *The Spectator*, March 1984, 31.
    Carpenter refers to the need for a new book "about the real Lewis and
    the presumptions upon which his reductive dogmatism was built."
 4. John Dart, "C. S. Lewis Honored in Church Window," *Los Angeles Times*,
    20 October 1984, sec. 2, p. 12. Dart describes the image of Lewis with
    academic gown, open book, and smoking pipe in hand.
 5. The property now distinguished by Lewis's thirty-three-year residence was
    long used as a quarry for a brick company. Removal of clay had created
    the pond that Lewis treasured. Lewis enjoyed the fact that according to
    local tradition the poet Shelley used to sail toy boats on this quarry pond.

    The house itself was built in 1922 and purchased by Lewis in 1930. It was
    named after the old brick furnaces that were finally demolished in 1964,
    shortly after Lewis's death. The Kilns Limited Partnership purchased the
    house in 1984 and made it a museum. In 1986 the partnership was turned
    into The Kilns Association, led by Paul F. Ford. The Association solicited
    subscriptions and lifetime memberships, the latter requiring a contribution
    of at least $2500. Plans for the Kilns included installation of a resident
    director, purchase of a house for the director to live in, purchase of other

houses in the neighborhood, computer equipment, library, and improvement of the property. Annual administrative costs alone for upkeep, interest on the mortgage, office supplies, printing, postage, and travel (apparently this refers to travel expenses of the resident director) were expected to average about $50,000 annually. These plans were far more ambitious than those of the original partnership.

Ralph Blair, founder of Evangelicals Concerned, reported near the end of 1987, "I was disappointed to find the Kilns overgrown with weeds and empty this summer while I was in Oxford."

6. The C. S. Lewis Institute was founded in 1976 by Dr. James M. Houston, also founder and former chancellor of Regent College in Vancouver, B.C. Dr. Houston earned his B.Sc., M.A., and D.Phil. at Oxford; he is former Bursar and Fellow of Hertford College and Lecturer in the University of Oxford; and he knew C. S. Lewis. The Institute offers biblical and theological studies on a modest scale. The mailing address is James R. Hiskey, 1904 N. Adams Street, Arlington, VA 22201.

7. Seattle Pacific University in Washington has repeatedly offered a summer C. S. Lewis conference with optional credit courses.

8. There are various ways to count Lewis's posthumous books, because of some overlap.

9. On 12 March 1979, at the Pasadena Civic Auditorium, Walter Hooper invited questions from the audience of over seven hundred. Douglas Hackleman of Grand Terrace, California, took the microphone and asked who makes the decisions for the C. S. Lewis estate concerning permissions and publications. Hooper answered emphatically, "I blush to answer: 'tis I." Since then the Curtis Brown agency of London has been involved also.

10. For an overview of Lewis's life, I particularly recommend his autobiographical *Surprised by Joy*; *And God Came In* by Lyle Dorsett; and *Jack: C. S. Lewis and His Times* by George B. Sayer. After those I recommend *C. S. Lewis, A Biography* by Roger Lancelyn Green and Walter Hooper; *The Inklings* by Humphrey Carpenter, and *C. S. Lewis: A Dramatic Life* by William Griffin.

11. Walter Cronkite stated, "The Chronicles of Narnia have genuine family appeal. In a dramatic and compelling way these classics present human values often lacking in today's television: loyalty, courage, caring, responsibility, truthfulness and compassion. Produced with care for these values, The Chronicles of Narnia can, and I believe will, become the classics in television that they are in literature."

When *The Lion, the Witch and the Wardrobe* appeared on television, it was reportedly viewed in 40 percent of American homes and in 63 percent of the homes with children between six and eleven years of age.

12. "C. S. Lewis Goes Marching On," *Time*, 5 December 1977, 92.

13. In my book *C. S. Lewis: Mere Christian* (Harold Shaw Publishers, 1987 edition) I first suggested that *The Dark Tower* was not by Lewis (pp. 195-96). "If truly written in 1938, this novel shows Lewis a bit ahead of his time in science fiction ideas. But if written around 1969 or later, as some readers suspect, *The Dark Tower* was derivative as well as a literary spoof. Thirty years make an immense difference."

14. C. S. Lewis, *The Weight of Glory* (New York: Macmillan, 1980), xi.
15. C. S. Lewis, *Boxen* (San Diego: Harcourt Brace Jovanovich, 1985), 18.
16. On 30 July 1965, in his first letter to me, Walter Hooper said, "Yes, I am an Anglican priest and it was my great pleasure to serve as honorary curate for a year in the parish church of which Lewis was a member."

    In fact, C. S. Lewis died 22 November 1963, and not until 27 September 1964 was Hooper ordained a deacon in the Diocese of Lexington, Kentucky (with the Bishop of Oxford acting for the Bishop of Lexington). Although Hooper's letter seemed to indicate that he had been an assistant priest for one year in the church in Headington Quarry where C. S. Lewis was worshipping before his death, in actuality he was a deacon at that church between 27 September 1964 and 27 June 1965, when *Warren* Lewis was worshipping there. For that story read chapter 8, "They Fall Together."
17. *The Canadian C. S. Lewis Journal*, April 1980, 8.
18. When some of these discrepancies were aired in 1979, Walter Hooper said to John Dart, religion editor of the *Los Angeles Times*, "There are 58 questions . . . and I am simply too busy to answer." "Questions Raised on C. S. Lewis Lore," *Los Angeles Times*, 24 March 1979, sec. 1, p. 30.
19. Clyde S. Kilby, *The Christian World of C. S. Lewis* (Grand Rapids, Mich.: Wm. B. Eerdmans Publishing Co., 1964), 5.

SHINING SOME LIGHT
ON THE
DARK TOWER

 How could a 1939 C. S. Lewis novel about time travel copy a scene from an American book that wasn't published until 1962? The mystery that shrouds *The Dark Tower* is more interesting than the ficto-science within it.

C. S. Lewis could enjoy a good hoax. He once enjoyed a hoax that attributed some American science fantasy to an eminent British astronomer. In 1957 C. S. Lewis thanked his friend Roger Lancelyn Green for a copy of Green's new book *Into Other Worlds*. The book tells about Lewis's own science fiction, and it is subtitled *Space Flights in Fiction from Lucian to Lewis*. What interested Lewis most in Green's book was the century-old story of the famous Lunar Hoax.[1]

In 1853 the New York *Sun* ran a series of scientific articles reprinted from the Edinburgh *Journal of Science*, a journal that never existed. The articles were alleged reports from the British astronomer Sir John Herschel, who had gone to the Cape of Good Hope to try out a powerful new telescope. Herschel's amazing descriptions of the moon fascinated readers. He described in colorful detail what he saw of oceans, beaches, plants, and even animals. Public excitement mounted with each new installment.

The fourth installment from Herschel described furry, bat-winged people who live on the moon. On the day that report was published, the *Sun* boasted the largest circulation of any paper in the world—19,360. Other papers were frantic and copied the articles from the *Sun*, claiming that they got them directly from the *Journal of Science*. A committee of suspicious scientists from Yale University hastened to New York to inspect the *Journal of Science* material; but the *Sun* shunted them here and there in their search for the missing document, and they finally gave up. At last, after three weeks, the *Sun* confessed its hoax.

An account of this great Lunar Hoax can be read in Curtis MacDougall's *Hoaxes* published in 1940 by Constable in England and by Macmillan in the United States, and now published by Dover Publications.[2]

C. S. Lewis thought the *Sun's* description of the moon's land and sea was remarkably well written, and he thought the hoax was good fun. It would no doubt have seemed incredible to Lewis that only nine years later he would be dead and a new book titled *Of Other Worlds* (Green's title was *Into Other Worlds*) would link his own science fiction novels to what seems to be a new hoax. This new hoax would not aim at selling a few thousand newspapers; it would aim at selling thousands of copies of a new book[3]—a book of science fiction purportedly by C. S. Lewis.

Lewis wrote three science fiction novels between 1937 and 1944. According to J. R. R. Tolkien, C. S. Lewis said to him one day, "Tollers, there is too little of what we really like in stories. I am afraid we shall have to try and write some ourselves." They agreed that Lewis would write of space travel and Tolkien would write of time travel.[4]

The two men were experienced readers of science fiction, but complete amateurs as writers of science fiction. Tolkien began to write a novel about the destruction of Atlantis, but his publisher told him that it would not be appealing enough to justify publication; he never finished it. Lewis forged ahead and finished his space novel, and then encountered difficulty in getting any publisher to accept it. After it was published in 1938 the reception was moderate until Lewis skyrocketed to popularity with his *Screwtape Letters* in 1942. From then on most Lewis fiction sold well.

This first science-fiction novel by Lewis, *Out of the Silent Planet*, told how a philology professor much like J. R. R. Tolkien was kidnapped by scoundrels and sent to Mars on their space ship. Through his surprising adventures there, the professor, Elwin Ransom, grew into a wise man and a hero in touch with the true meaning of the universe.

Not all science-fiction enthusiasts enjoy *Out of the Silent Planet*, partly because it includes nothing about technology or science and is in reality a moral and religious fantasy. But many agree with Marjorie Nicolson, author of the historical study *Voyages to the Moon*. She declared at the end of her book, "*Out of the Silent Planet* is to me the most beautiful of all cosmic voyages and in some ways the most moving."[5]

In the second of the series, *Perelandra* (1943), Ransom

left the earth for Venus and entered into the cosmic struggle between good and evil there. In this book Lewis dispensed with a spaceship altogether and transported Ransom in a mysterious white coffinlike box. *Perelandra* is a spiritual thriller with scenes of breathtaking beauty. It has been the favorite Lewis book of many Lewis readers, and was reportedly his own favorite of all his books.

The third book of the trilogy, *That Hideous Strength* (1945), engaged Ransom in a struggle against cosmic evil here on earth. Merlin came back to life to help; and, quite literally, hell broke loose and the heavens came down to earth. For all the outer tumult and cataclysm, the main adventure was inner again.

Needless to say, those who love this trilogy have often wished that Lewis had written a tetralogy instead. Twenty-one years after *That Hideous Strength* was published, they were told that they had not wished in vain. There *was* a fourth Lewis novel about Ransom's adventures!

It was in 1966 that two sentences in the preface of the new Lewis anthology *Of Other Worlds* quietly announced that this unknown novel existed.[6] C. S. Lewis had been dead three years when the news came out. Excited inquiries brought forth no information, and so there was nothing for Lewis enthusiasts to do but to wait hopefully.

Eight years later, eager readers finally found a preview of the fourth Ransom novel in the Lewis biography *C. S. Lewis: A Biography* by Roger Lancelyn Green and Walter Hooper.[7] Green announced that the fourth novel was, in fact, only part of a novel. After eight years of suspense, that belated announcement was a severe disappointment. But Green's evaluation of the fragment was at least as disappointing as the news that the novel was only half written. Green did not praise it.

Roger Lancelyn Green was a meticulous and dependable literary scholar, and he was a friend of C. S. Lewis for many years. He began his review of the strange newly-revealed fragment by noting that no one from the past, not even Lewis's brother, had ever seen or heard of this aborted manuscript while Lewis was alive.[8] Furthermore, Lewis never mentioned the project in any of his letters to friends. This was completely unlike Lewis's behavior when he wrote the other three Ransom novels, which his friends were well aware of at the time of the writing.

Green summarized the plot for the public. The story is told by C. S. Lewis this time, as an active participant in the story. (In the other three Ransom novels Lewis merely related the stories as they had been told to him by his friend Ransom.) The story begins in the Cambridge room of Dr. Orfieu, with his assistant Scudamour, C. S. Lewis, Ransom, and MacPhee there. (MacPhee is an instructor from Manchester University who appears as a far more interesting and lifelike character in *That Hideous Strength*.) This group looks into a "chronoscope," which shows with three-dimensional realism what is transpiring in some other time—not necessarily past or present, and most likely another time system parallel to ours.

The friends see inside a dark tower in which an extremely sinister man sits and waits for ordinary humans to come to him to be destroyed. The man has an oozing growth on his forehead like an oversized red thorn, and he plunges it into the spines of his semi-naked victims, making them into zombies. Scudamour's double appears in the pictures, and this double grows a sting on his forehead. Then the double of Scudamour's fiancée Camilla appears and is about to be stabbed in the spine by him. The real Scudamour breaks the chronoscope in a fit of rage, and thus accidentally trades bodies with his double, acquiring the sting on his forehead and finding himself in Othertime.

From that point on, the last quarter of the manuscript consists of Scudamour describing his adventures in Othertime. The last section is "an over-long and laboured account" of Othertime mathematics and science that Scudamour reads about in a library there. It is an amazingly long, difficult, inappropriate passage to find in a C. S. Lewis novel. The story breaks off in midsentence at that point, before getting back to its characters.

According to Green, there is yet no clue to the real content of the book. One can only guess at what Lewis had in mind. The slowness of the connecting links and sheer lifelessness of Scudamour's investigations suggest to Green that Lewis discarded the book because he had no idea what should happen next.

Hoping that Green was unduly grim about the quality of the fourth novel, those who had read his description tended to want to see for themselves. Three years later, in 1977, Collins in England and Harcourt Brace Jovanovich in the United States published *The Dark Tower and Other Stories*. (All but one of its other stories were already available in *Of Other Worlds*.) The attraction of this volume was obviously the mysterious *Dark Tower* fragment pictured on the cover. The book is in public and private libraries all over Britain and the United States, and it is still selling. That does not mean that it is being read.[9]

As published, *The Dark Tower* is preceded and followed by ten pages of notes that seek to tell us all about it. The original manuscript is described as yellow with age. It consists of sixty-two pages of lined paper measuring 8.5 inches by 13 inches. Pages 11 and 49 are missing, and the last page is numbered 64. Lewis's handwriting is clearly legible.

The notes claim that *The Dark Tower* was hinted at by Lewis in the last sentence of *Out of the Silent Planet*, which indicates that with the destruction of the earth's only spaceship, the characters would have to travel back in time to use that spaceship in a sequel. I find the connection of that sentence to *The Dark Tower* less than persuasive. No one goes back in time in *The Dark Tower*, and there is no hint of a spaceship. The claim that *Out of the Silent Planet* points toward *The Dark Tower* is a bewildering one.

The notes also point out that one character in *The Dark Tower* conveniently stressed that they were living in 1938, which shows that Lewis wrote *The Dark Tower* in 1938. Lewis's other novels do not offer readers such tips about when they were written.

The notes claim that although "it would be madness to put such literature on a level with Scripture, and unwisdom to mistake it for the advancement of an ethical theorem," it is a pleasure to offer it as good holiday fiction for entertainment. It should not be compared with Lewis's other science fiction. Even Lewis himself did not believe it attained that level of perfection. In fact, the notes remark, Lewis probably did not remember that he had written it.[10]

In the biography, Green had claimed that no one else remembered the story either, but the notes correct that mistake. They explain that Lewis's friend Gervase Mathew had indeed heard Lewis read the first four chapters of this novel aloud at an Inklings meeting in 1939 or 1940. Some of the unnamed friends who heard it along with Mathew complained to Lewis that the sting seemed to have unpleasant sexual connotations which Lewis did not intend. Mathew and Lewis discussed the novel again as they strolled around Addison's Walk at Magdalen College. Unfortunately for curious or skeptical readers, Gervase Mathew was dead by the time *The Dark Tower* was published and could not be reached for comment; there is no way to check the claim that the dying Mathew remembered hearing Lewis read *The Dark Tower*. Some readers have been puzzled by the Mathew account. If Lewis was warned by friends wiser than he that the sexual symbolism of the sting was too obvious, why did he go ahead and use it even more graphically in chapter 5? There Scudamour gained relief by stinging his hand in a startling parody of masturbation.

The Dark Tower has been an embarrassment to friendly C. S. Lewis critics; many of them simply ignore it. In 1979 in *The Literary Legacy of C. S. Lewis*, Chad Walsh exclaimed that it is hard to imagine a book less like its predecessor.[11] *Out of the Silent Planet* had plausible characters, color, vivid scenes, and strong goodness as well as evil. In *The Dark Tower* the characters are all dull and colorless. The story is talky. There are long paragraphs of pseudoscientific jargon. The tale is unpleasant, rather morbid, and without any apparent meaning.

In 1981, in *C. S. Lewis: The Art of Enchantment*, Donald Glover also emphasized the sharp contrast between *Out of the Silent Planet* and *The Dark Tower*.[12] In the latter the interest seems to be more scientific and mechanical than imaginative. It is stiff and slow in narration, thin in descriptive matter, and heavy with "information."

In 1981, in Ungar's *C. S. Lewis*, Margaret Hannay voiced some of these same criticisms, adding the problem of the overly obvious and unpleasant sexual implications of the sting.[13] Hannay also pointed out that the control of the Big Brain over those who have been stung is remark-ably similar to the control that IT exercised over its victims in Madeleine L'Engle's classic children's book *A Wrinkle in Time*, which was not published until 1962. L'Engle, on the other hand, could not have been influenced by *The Dark Tower*, because she published her fantasy in 1962, and she could not have seen *The Dark Tower* until 1977. Hannay did not consider the far-fetched possibility that *The Dark Tower* was really written after 1963, when *A Wrinkle in Time* won the Newbery Award and became an instant favorite with the reading public.

If one wanted to guess at a date of composition for *The Dark Tower* after 1963, when Lewis died, it would make sense to set it sometime between the 1966 announcement of a fourth Ransom novel (not identified as a fragment) and the accurate description of the fragment published in 1974 by Roger Lancelyn Green. With such a scenario in mind, it is worth looking at the similarity between the zombie accounts in the two books.

In *A Wrinkle in Time*, L'Engle wrote, "As they approached the end of the room their steps slowed. Before them was a platform. On the platform was a chair, and on the chair was a man."[14] Something about the man was intensely cold and dark.

In *The Dark Tower*, one reads that there was a dais at the front of the room. By it there was a chair, and on it sat the Man. He was singularly unattractive, with a mass of black hair that was dead black, with the blackness of a coal cellar (page 31).

Standing before the seated man in *A Wrinkle in Time*, Charles Wallace was taken over by the man's power; and then he gave his sister a smile that was not his smile. When he was told to go, he started to walk in a strange mechanical manner. He walked out of the room with a jerky rhythm and did not look back to see if the others were coming (page 137). He had a marionette's walk (page 138). He moved jerkily (page 139).

Standing before the seated Man in *The Dark Tower*, a beautiful young man was taken over by the power of the Man; and then his face wore a fixed grin. When he was to go, he did not look behind him at the one who had stung him. He strutted with sharp, jerky movements, as if marching strangely to some abominable music. All individuals left that room with a permanent clockwork swagger (page 35). C. S. Lewis, the narrator in the story, said that he and his friends called these slaves "Jerkies."

Perhaps someone who had read *A Wrinkle in Time* wrote *The Dark Tower* as an apocryphal C. S. Lewis story. The almost unrelieved nastiness of the book seems a blemish on Lewis's character, and the inferior writing (produced between *Out of the Silent Planet* and *The Problem of Pain*) seems a blemish on his otherwise stable intellect. On 7 July 1986, Lewis's friend Sheldon Vanauken wrote to me, "I dislike TDT, wish it had been burnt if his, and would be glad to have it proved a fraud."

Madeleine L'Engle herself has been disturbed by the seeming likeness between *The Dark Tower* and her Camazotz scenes in *A Wrinkle in Time*.[15] She cannot account for the similarity. But she wrote her book as an affirmation of a God of particularity and love, and *The Dark Tower* has no such affirmation.

In fact, *The Dark Tower* never seems to rise above Scudamour's belief, "Some filthy sort of something going on alongside the ordinary world and all mixed up with it" (page 48). That sentence strikes me as an ominous summary of the whole *Dark Tower* affair.

A scenario that would absolve Lewis of responsibility for *The Dark Tower* and account for most of the circumstances was once suggested to me by Vanauken.[16] Perhaps around 1950, after Lewis's space trilogy was familiar to the public, one of Lewis's students or correspondents tried writing a fourth book for the series. He included C. S. Lewis and MacPhee from *That Hideous Strength*, and the others. Lewis kept the unfinished attempt among his papers as a curiosity, unidentified.

After Lewis's death, Walter Hooper found this manuscript among papers he saved from a bonfire; because the penmanship resembled that of C. S. Lewis, he mistook it for Lewis's handwriting. Later, shortly before the death of Lewis's old friend Gervase Mathew, this seriously ill man mistakenly thought he recalled Lewis reading the story aloud in 1939.

As far-fetched as this scenario is, it seems far more likely than the idea that C. S. Lewis wrote *The Dark Tower*. All it leaves out is *A Wrinkle in Time*.

Ironically, a similar scenario turned out to be true for a lost Sherlock Holmes story discovered by Adrian Conan Doyle in a chest of his father's papers in 1942. The whole affair is now described by Richard Lancelyn Green, son of C. S. Lewis's friend and biographer Roger Lancelyn Green, in his 1985 book *The Further Adventures of Sherlock Holmes*.[17]

In 1911 a Holmes enthusiast named Arthur Whitaker submitted his story "The Man Who Was Wanted" to Arthur Conan Doyle, who paid him ten guineas for it and filed it as a possible source of story ideas for future use. In 1942 Adrian came across it and announced the discovery to an eager world of Holmes readers. Adrian gave the impression that the manuscript was in his father's handwriting, although in fact it was in typescript. He allowed his father's biographer Hesketh Pearson to quote from the story in his 1943 volume about Conan Doyle;

this foreshadowed biographer Roger Lancelyn Green being allowed to introduce *The Dark Tower* in his 1974 volume about C. S. Lewis. (Green, who knew Lewis's handwriting well, saw only a typescript of *The Dark Tower*.) Neither Green nor Pearson doubted the authenticity of these manuscripts.

The apocryphal Conan Doyle story was published with fanfare in *Cosmopolitan* in the United States in August 1948, and published in the *Sunday Dispatch* in England in January 1949. The editor explained that Conan Doyle and his family realized that this story was not up to his usual standard, but that the family now yielded to public pressure to publish it anyway. This was meant to forestall criticism, but it didn't work.

Some serious Sherlock Holmes experts didn't believe that the story was genuine Conan Doyle and said so in print. One suspected Adrian of concocting it, one suspected Adrian and his brother Dennis of constructing it from notes left by their father, and another suspected that it was by an American forger. In fact, the real writer of the story had tried to identify himself in 1945, when he happened to discover the mistake in Pearson's biography of Conan Doyle, but to no avail.

When Whitaker realized that his old story was now published in its entirety under the name of Conan Doyle, he wrote to the Conan Doyle sons about it in January 1949. To his surprise, he received an angry reply from Adrian threatening to sue him for casting aspersion on the manuscript. Indeed, Adrian turned the matter over to Vertue, Son & Churcher, solicitors for the Conan Doyle estate. He seemed eager for a fight.

Whitaker called in his own solicitors, provided them with his 1911 letter from Conan Doyle about the manuscript, and promptly settled the matter; then he promptly died. If he had died one year sooner, "The Man Who Was Wanted" might have remained in the Conan Doyle corpus until this day. It lasted in the corpus seven years.

So far *The Dark Tower* has been included in the Lewis corpus for over twenty years, and no one has come forth and confessed writing it yet. Hope for that grows fainter every year.

When Arthur C. Clarke, who was C. S. Lewis's own favorite science-fiction author, heard about the problem of *The Dark Tower*, he said, "I would like to see justice done, and this is certainly an intriguing case."[18] (Clarke had an extensive correspondence with Lewis, and was also a friend of Joy Lewis.)[19]

Carla Faust Jones, a graduate student at the University of Florida, took an interest in this puzzle in 1986 and tried her hand at a computer analysis of the prose in *The Dark Tower*, *Out of the Silent Planet*, *Perelandra*, and *That Hideous Strength*. She found some difference between *The Dark Tower* and the other three with regard to letter frequencies, which simply showed that *The Dark Tower* was a divergence from Lewis's normal style. Unfortunately, she had to return to her academic program in her own subject area and has not been able to pursue the topic beyond her preliminary study.[20]

Lacking a computer with which to measure the quantity of factors in different pieces of literature, readers can resort to sensing the quality of different pieces of literature with their own brains, as C. S. Lewis would have done. One can look for the style, cadence, content, moral character, and philosophical or religious tone. Those who do this with *The Dark Tower* usually conclude "I cannot prove that this is not by Lewis, but much of it does not seem at all like Lewis's writing to me."

Lewis's sentences are noted for their grace and vitality.

Yet *The Dark Tower* includes wordy sentences like this one: "What followed has effaced it, for destiny chose this night to pitchfork us brutally, and with no gentle grada- tions, into something so shocking that, if I had not had the business of recording it always before my mind, it would by now perhaps have been dropped out of my consciousness altogether." It was by never writing such turgid prose that Lewis achieved his vigorous style.

Lewis had an attitude toward sexuality that was neither prudish nor sniggering; it could most simply be called a "clean-minded" approach, including awe, humor, and humility about temptation. He did not avoid or stress sex in his writing. Yet in *The Dark Tower* he supposedly wrote, "During the whole of our stay in College with Orfieu, his aged colleague Knellie (Cyril Knellie, the now almost forgotten author of *Erotici Graeci Minimi*, *Table Talk of a Famous Courtesan*, and *Lesbos: A Masque*) was a great trial to us." The old reprobate, who combines a senile, spinsterish personality with an unquenchable appetite for filth, seems gratuitous to the plot. But Lewis or the unknown author seems to take glee in writing about him. It seems unlike Lewis to afflict his readers with such humor.

Lewis, for all his humor and humility, had personal dignity appropriate to an Oxford don. Yet as the author of *The Dark Tower* he put into his own mouth as a char- acter in the story the following sentence: "On the strength of having been at my old college—some time in the nineties—he addressed me as Lu-Lu, a sobriquet I particu- larly dislike." It seems highly unlikely that Lewis would choose to have anyone call him Lu-Lu in a novel; he might have been mocked that way from then on. Further- more, aside from Lu-Lu, Lewis would particularly dislike in his own prose the phrase "a sobriquet I particularly dislike." He never used words that could give the impression of prissy fastidiousness. He would have been apt to write simply, "I loathe that name." One odd sentence cannot prove a point, but perhaps dozens of them can. *The Dark Tower* has dozens of sentences that are odd indeed.

Here are some sample sentences, in chronological order, from *The Dark Tower* with criticisms that C. S. Lewis might be apt to make if he read them:

> The jibe recalled Orfieu to the real purpose of our meeting, and after a few moments of keen but not unkindly chaff between the two philosophers we settled ourselves to listen again. (Page 19.)
> *Stodgy narrative.*

> "Um—well perhaps," said Orfieu. (Page 20.) "All right, all right," said Orfieu with a smile. (Page 25.)
> *Slow dialogue.*

> I think that all of us, even MacPhee, were a bit excited by now, and we urged Orfieu to go on with his demonstration. (Page 25.)
> *Plodding style.*

> "Is it in the future or the past?" I queried. (Page 27.)
> *Amateurish verb choice.*

> It was hard and horny, but not like a bone. It was red, like most of the things in a man, and apparently lubricated by some kind of saliva. (Page 33.)
> *Accidental vulgarity.*

> We realized afresh that behind certain windows, not fifty yards away, humanity was opening a door that had been sealed from the beginning, and that a train of consequences incalculable for good or evil was on foot. (Page 29.)
> *Mixed metaphors.*

To us, of course, the whole Othertime world was absolutely silent: in reality, what between the bands and the noise of the workmen, it must have been dinning with sound. (Page 40.)
Superfluous words "what" and "with sound."

I remember Ransom saying, "That young fellow may blow up any moment." (Page 44.)
Inappropriate dialogue.

At this point it will be convenient if my narrative turns to Scudamour. (Page 61.)
Awkward transitional sentence.

At this time he did not, of course, understand the linguistic situation which I have just described. (Page 65.)
Wordiness and awkward transition.

But he felt that he was now very nearly at the end of his tether. (Page 77.)
Cliche.

Presumably the body which Scudamour now animated had not fed for some time, and he found himself turning to his meal with alacrity. (Page 79.)
Circuitous and stilted style.

"I don't believe a word of it!" ejaculated Scudamour suddenly . . . (Page 87.)
Poor verb choice with superfluous adverb.

Most of these sentence weaknesses are minor flaws that occur frequently in the prose of ordinary writers. But they are completely out of character for C. S. Lewis, who was no ordinary writer.

In conclusion, *The Dark Tower* looks like a hoax because it is vastly inferior to all of Lewis's authentic fiction;

it has not been demonstrated that anyone ever heard of it while Lewis was alive; it includes a suspicious echo of the 1962 children's classic *A Wrinkle in Time*; and it is dissimilar to Lewis's other writing in style, content, and sexual orientation. None of these facts alone can prove that *The Dark Tower* is a hoax; but, taken together, they are extremely strong evidence. There is so far no apparent evidence on the other side.

For people who took *The Dark Tower* seriously and now decide that it must be a hoax, some words on page 45 take on a special meaning. There the skeptical Mac-Phee scolds Orfieu for trying to get him to believe in the chronoscope: "you can have your joke—but I'm not going to stay here and be hoaxed any longer." The author, whoever he is, has said it for us.[21]

But what about the yellowed, sixty-two-page manuscript in Lewis's own handwriting? Doesn't it prove that *The Dark Tower* is genuine?[22] The story of the mysterious *Dark Tower* manuscript is, in fact, the story of the famous C. S. Lewis bonfire. That is the subject of chapter 3.

Chapter 2, Notes
 1. Roger Lancelyn Green and Walter Hooper, *C. S. Lewis: A Biography* (London: Collins, 1974), 163.
 2. Curtis D. MacDougall, *Hoaxes* (New York: Dover, 1958), 229- 31.
 3. In *C. S. Lewis: The Man and His Achievements* (Exeter, England: The Paternoster Press, 1985). John Peters says Lewis books sell almost 2 million copies yearly in Britain and the U. S. alone. Lyle Dorsett of the Wade Center at Wheaton College says the actual figures are not made available from the publishers; he has estimated 1.5 million copies or more.
 4. Humphrey Carpenter, *Tolkien* (Boston: Houghton Mifflin, 1977), 170.
 5. As quoted by Green and Hooper in *C. S. Lewis*, 165.
 6. C. S. Lewis, *Of Other Worlds* (New York: Harcourt Brace Jovanovich, 1966), viii.
 7. Green and Hooper, *C. S. Lewis*, 166-69.
 8. Ibid., 166.
 9. On 31 January 1987, Lewis's friend Charles Wrong wrote to me, "I have to confess I started it but didn't finish it. I think it's the only Lewis book

of which this is true." On 12 June 1987, Lewis's friend Dom Bede Griffiths wrote to me, "I have got a copy of *The Dark Tower* but I have not read it. It didn't attract me." These seem to be typical reactions.

10. C. S. Lewis, *The Dark Tower and Other Stories* ed. Walter Hooper (New York: Harcourt Brace Jovanovich, 1977), 9.

11. Chad Walsh, *The Literary Legacy of C. S. Lewis* (New York: Harcourt Brace Jovanovich, 1979), 96-98.

12. Donald E. Glover, *C. S. Lewis: The Art of Enchantment* (Athens, Ohio: Ohio University Press, 1981), 85-91.

13. Margaret Patterson Hannay, *C. S. Lewis* (New York: Frederick Ungar Publishing Co., 1981), 252-54.

14. Madeleine L'Engle, *A Wrinkle in Time* (New York: Farrar, Straus and Giroux, 1962; Dell Edition, 1973), 120.

15. Madeleine L'Engle, personal letter to me, 17 February 1987.

16. Sheldon Vanauken, personal letter to me, 27 February 1987.

17. Published by Penguin Books in 1985. See pages 13-19.

18. Arthur C. Clarke, personal letter to me, 18 February 1987 from his home in Sri Lanka. On 20 July 1956, Lewis remarked to me in conversation that Arthur C. Clarke was his favorite science fiction author.

19. On 22 December 1953, C. S. Lewis wrote to Joy Davidman about Arthur C. Clarke's science fiction, "It [*Childhood's End*] is quite out of the range of the common space-and-time writers. . . . It is better than any of Stapledon's. It hasn't got Ray Bradbury's delicacy, but then it has ten times his emotional power, and far more mythopoeia." As quoted by Glover in *Art of Enchantment*, 38.

20. Jones made use of the Literary Detective computer program in her study, and her results were confirmed by the author of that program. In her report she does not seek to justify the Literary Detective as a legitimate indicator of a writer's style, which would be beyond the scope of her project. Her personal response to the import of her study, stated in a letter 10 December 1987, was "I'm certainly excited about all of this and am rather astounded that I was able to participate in such a literary mystery. Little did I know what was beginning when I placed a rose on Lewis's grave in 1977."

21. In 1986 Roger Lancelyn Green, then sixty-eight years old, had never yet doubted that *The Dark Tower* was written by C. S. Lewis (according to a letter dated September 30). But in May or June 1987, he read an early draft of this book at one sitting and apparently changed his mind. His only general criticism was that chapter 9 (what is now appendix 1) was anticlimactic; he thought chapter 8 would make a better ending. He said he found little to fault and much that he agreed with. He sent his thanks and appreciation on June 6. On October 8 he died.

22. Professor Edgar L. Chapman of Bradley University in Peoria, Illinois, proposed in a letter in the October 1979 issue of *Mythlore*, "The best thing for Father Hooper to do to restore trust would be to make the unpublished version of the Lewis papers already published available to the public and to other Lewis scholars so that his work as an editor can be evaluated. . . . Silence is not the answer." The answer was silence.

3.

THROWING WATER ON THE BONFIRE STORY

The Lewis Bonfire story is both heart-rending and heart-warming.[1] Disaster followed disaster when C. S. Lewis died. Within two months his disconsolate brother, "the Major," went on an erratic housecleaning binge and dumped out pile after pile of precious Lewis papers and manuscripts. Relentlessly, he passed bushels of papers on to Fred Paxford, the old gardener, to be thrown on a hungry bonfire in the orchard.

All day long flames licked the sheaves of paper covered with Lewis's small, tidy penmanship; all the white pages curled, and browned, and charred, and turned to fine white ash. Smoke rose through the bare branches of surrounding trees hour after hour, drifting away toward the winter sky. Flakes of ash sometimes swirled up in a gust of breeze like ghosts of the words and ideas that Lewis had laboriously entrusted to paper with his old-fashioned broad-nibbed pen. Sounds of crackling flame and rushing air were the last sounds those words would ever make; and their many meanings all became just one meaning: *Lost*. It has been claimed that some of the pages that burned contained Lewis's continuation of his autobiography *Surprised by Joy*, telling the story of the second half of his life.[2] No one ever got to read it.

Faithful Paxford, straining and shuffling a bit, silently heaved another batch of pages onto the fire. After thirty-three years of tending the grounds of the Lewis home, he sorely missed "the Boss." First, the real boss, Mrs. Moore, had died of old age in 1951. Then before long Joy Davidman, an American, arrived on the scene and became Mrs. Lewis. But she didn't last long; she was soon dead of cancer. And now, three years later, the Boss himself was dead. Only the Major was left here now, with neighbors Len and Mollie Miller to look after him. And the American stepsons would come home between terms sometimes. How short life's good years seem when we look back, Paxford probably reflected sadly. And the days are short in January England. Sundown before 5:00 p.m. Six hours of burning done already, and a small mountain of paper still left for tomorrow's flames.

The second day was like the first. Morning, afternoon, and evening, Fred Paxford dutifully tended the Major's fire in the orchard, burning papers and manuscripts whose value will never be known. When night fell, fuel for several more hours was left.

On the third morning Paxford started the bonfire again. But he got an idea. This time he begged the Major for permission to set aside a large quantity of notebooks and manuscripts that might be of special value. Paxford had got the idea of showing them to an American man who had just moved to Oxford and was living in a spare room at Keble College. The Major relented; Paxford could save that pile of papers for Walter Hooper, but only until sundown. If Hooper did not arrive before then and carry them away, they would have to be burned at sundown.

Before long, Walter Hooper got a peculiar feeling that he must visit the Lewis home that very day, no matter what. Not knowing why, he went there in the afternoon. As he was walking up the drive, Fred Paxford came to meet him and steered him to the fire in the orchard. The pile of notebooks and manuscripts that had appealed to Paxford was right there waiting for him. Did he want it? It took all of stouthearted Hooper's strength and energy to carry the huge pile back to his room by means of two large trunks and a city bus. He got back at suppertime.

As soon as possible after supper, Hooper rushed to his room to examine his windfall. Among many other things, he found a blue notebook full of poems, a yellowed manuscript of a science fiction novel about a dark tower, and some of Lewis's childhood writing and drawing. Although he was living among many good friends of C. S. Lewis, he did not tell anyone about the rescue of "a pile of scorched manuscripts," as he referred to them later. The bonfire remained his secret for over ten years.

According to Hooper, the Major never admitted to himself or others what he had done. As a lifelong bachelor who was devoted to his famous brother and who cherished every scrap of Lewis data, this sensitive and sentimental man could not face the fact of his own destructiveness.

In March of 1964, less than two months after the three-day bonfire, Major Lewis was himself again and advertising in England and the United States for any letters from C. S. Lewis that people could contribute to the book of Lewis letters that he was working on. In

April he was responding clearly and in detail to people who wanted to contribute.[3]

After the book of letters finally came out, the Major wrote to me, "I am glad that you enjoyed the 'Letters.' Putting them together was an interesting but sad task for me. I was much touched by the extraordinarily generous response from America to my appeal for material, and particularly from those who sent photostats, saying they would not trust the originals out of their possession.

"I am glad you liked the photos. Personally, I always fight rather shy of this kind of book if I find it is not illustrated."[4]

After reading my review of his book, he wrote again:

Many thanks for sending me your very interesting and understanding article on my collection of the C. S. L. letters—and your overflattering reference to 'the highly gifted writer' who did the arranging of them! Most of us produce books these days to help pay our taxes, but in this case I felt that firstly, such a collection was a debt owing to my brother's memory, and secondly that letters which had been of such value to their recipients might easily benefit a larger circle. In the latter object I am proud to say that I've been successful, and letters have poured in from all quarters thanking me for having published. He himself would have enjoyed your well-written tribute.

As regards the length of the book, don't blame me, but the publisher who for commercial reasons cut out all the material I had supplied for the first fifteen years of my brother's life—a mistake, I thought, for when I read a book of this sort it is the childhood and boyish years which always seem to me the most interesting.[5]

Well before his own death, Major Lewis had arranged for all his own collection of Lewis papers and manuscripts to go to Dr. Clyde S. Kilby's collection at Wheaton College in Illinois (now called the Marion E. Wade Center) for public use.

The Major died in 1973, and in the 1974 biography of C. S. Lewis, Walter Hooper finally allowed the world to find out about *The Dark Tower* fragment, although he was not yet ready to tell who had it or where he got it. (The biography not only failed to mention the juvenilia rescued from the same fire, but denied the existence of such juvenilia. Hooper was to reveal the existence of rescued juvenilia later.) On 16 August 1975, guest-of-honor Hooper told the bonfire story to an enthralled audience in California;[6] and in 1977 he published it in his preface to *The Dark Tower* and told it to enthralled audiences in both London and New York.[7] He even said the bonfire was an essential episode in his becoming literary executor for C. S. Lewis's estate.

Shortly after the bonfire story was published in *The Dark Tower*, word of it got to Len Miller and Fred Paxford, who were appalled. "As regards Walter Hooper's story about a bonfire, I am still in touch with Paxford and went to see him yesterday," Len Miller wrote to me. "He says it is all lies."[8]

According to Miller and Paxford, early in 1964 the Major had Paxford burn some worthless papers that he and Lewis's lawyer Owen Barfield had carefully sorted out. But those papers were not literature, and they did not make a three-day fire. Moreover, Fred Paxford did not ask for permission to set anything aside for the young American. He simply burned the trash and was done with it. It boggled his mind to be told fourteen years later that he had been the hero who rescued a pile of valuable manuscripts. Nonsense, he answered.[9]

It is often said that dour, honest Fred Paxford inspired

C. S. Lewis to invent Puddleglum, the Marshwiggle, in *The Silver Chair* of the Narnian Chronicles. It happens that Puddleglum's finest hour came when he broke the magic spell caused by a sweet-smelling fire; he stamped it out with his bare feet and woke everyone up. That's one of the high points in the Narnian Chronicles. Perhaps Paxford's flat-footed denial of the enchanting bonfire story gives him more in common with Puddleglum than anyone could have foreseen.

When Paxford's denial was published in *Christianity & Literature*, a small journal for American instructors of literature, it created almost as much heat as the famous bonfire. Several angry letters came in protesting the publication of "tasteless probing." But one of the letters that came in seemed positive. It came from a scientist in England. The editor of *Christianity & Literature* was much interested and published it in the Winter 1979 issue.[10]

The bonfire letter was typed on official letterhead stationery of the Physical Chemistry Laboratory of Oxford University, on South Parks Road, Oxford OX1 3OZ. The letterhead includes the traditional Oxford shield with three crowns surrounding an open book with the Latin inscription on it "Dominus Illuminatio Mea" ("the Lord is my light"). The letter was dated 20 November 1978. It began with the title *Carbon Particle Analysis: A Fresh Dimension to the Lewis Bonfire*: A contribution to the productive dialogue from Anthony Marchington, B.A. (Oxon), of the Physical Chemistry Laboratory, Oxford, England. Marchington states:

> Far be it from me to involve myself in an ongoing situation of debate, but I wish simply to report here, without any malice or prejudice, the results of scientific research carried out here in Oxford over the last three years which, I believe, goes a long way in answering the question: "Did the bonfire of

C. S. Lewis's papers which Hooper claims to have witnessed ever actually occur?" and if so, "Do the remains of this bonfire under chemical analysis account for all the papers which Hooper claims were destroyed?"

A collaborative research project between the University departments of Chemistry and Archeology has recently given birth to a new method of dating sites of pyrolitic residue. The minute details of this research needn't be explained here, but in order to interpret the results a short description must be given.

Basically, during a bonfire fine particulate carbon along with refractory ash and minerals are deposited about the site. Much of the surface material is then dispersed by the elements but a representative insoluble sample remains indefinitely at various depths in the soil. The carbon trapped as fine particles in this ash has been the subject of our research. Firstly, its chemical analysis can tell us what sort of material was originally burned: e.g. wood, paper, leather etc. This sort of analysis is now standard practice. Secondly, however, our work at Oxford has shown that computer structural data analysis of particle sizes can yield both date and average temperature of such a bonfire. Of our many recent successes I can quote the application of this technique to earth excavated from a place close to the main lectern in the old Coventry Cathedral, England. As a result we were able to pinpoint the remains of what was most likely the Cathedral Bible and calculated the date of its burning as between May and December 1940. The night of the Coventry Blitz when the Old Cathedral was destroyed was, in fact, 14 November 1940. Encouraged by such results and others we are at present applying this new method to many such fires of historical interest.

This letter goes on to say that some of Marchington's research workers went to Hooper's apartment to discuss plans for analysis of the Lewis bonfire over tea, and Hooper's response to the project was "Professional scientists ought to have better things to do than rummaging around in soot." In fact, that opinion of his was published in the University newspaper.

Marchington goes on to describe the process of obtaining soil samples from about a third of an acre around the site of the reported bonfire and transporting thirteen hundred pounds—over a half-ton—of soil from Lewis's orchard to the laboratory. There the soil was examined with standard methods such as Light Interferometry, Ultra Violet Spectroscopy, and Combustion Elemental Analysis. This analysis proved that there had not been a significant bonfire of any sort in that area for at least eight hundred years.

The letter is signed by Anthony F. Marchington, Hulme Exhibitioner and Charitable Foundation Scholar, Brasenose College, Oxford. In a note at the bottom of the page, he says, "As with all my publications, a copy of this article has been given to my academic supervisor, Dr. Stephen C. F. Moore (Brasenose College) and to Dr. T. G. Earp (Malvern) to whom I am greatly indebted."

Although many readers were immensely impressed with this research, a little transatlantic detective work revealed that Marchington's "academic supervisor, Dr. Stephen C. F. Moore" was in fact just a young science student. More important, many readers declared that the letter was a silly batch of ficto-science, not real science at all.[11]

Furthermore, without the help of Light Interferometry or Ultra Violet Spectroscopy—just an ordinary magnifying glass—I discovered that although Marchington's letter was typed on official stationery of Oxford University's Physical Chemistry Laboratory, it was not typed there. It was typed on Walter Hooper's own home typewriter. The minute irregularities in the letter configurations make that indisputable. Marchington's letter was typed on the same machine that Walter Hooper used for his own typing for years.[12]

The fact that Marchington pretended in his letter that he did not know Hooper and sent researchers to Hooper's apartment to discuss the project with him takes on a new light when one guesses that Marchington was typing that very letter in Hooper's apartment, probably chuckling.

There can be no question. The Marchington "Lewis Bonfire" letter is a practical joke. To this day I do not know why Anthony Marchington wrote the bonfire letter. Friends of mine suggested that he might have expected me to take the letter seriously and stake my reputation on it. Then he could have exposed my gullibility and discredited me by explaining his joke. I have since written to Marchington in care of Walter Hooper but received no reply. I wish he had answered.

If it is true that *The Dark Tower* was not written by C. S. Lewis and was not rescued from the three-day bonfire by Fred Paxford and Walter Hooper, then *The Dark Tower* and the bonfire story and the bonfire letter look like parts of an audacious hoax.

Who could have written *The Dark Tower*? No one thinks that Walter Hooper could have tackled all that ficto-science. The most obvious suspect is Anthony Marchington himself. He is a scientist, he is interested in the origin of *The Dark Tower*, and he has tricked *Christianity & Literature* with a scientific spoof. Furthermore, he was about eight years old when Madeleine L'Engle published her children's classic *A Wrinkle in Time*, and so he quite possibly read it as a child. That could account for unconscious copying of L'Engle's automaton scene in *The Dark Tower*. It all fits almost too neatly.

How did Anthony Marchington get involved in C. S. Lewis affairs, and what else has he written? That is the subject of chapter 4.

Chapter 3, Notes

1. Walter Hooper has told the story in introductions to *The Dark Tower*, *They Stand Together*, and *Boxen*. He told it in the 1977 April and August issues of the bulletin *CSL*. And he has told it in *Alumni Review* of the University of North Carolina in March 1980 (pp. 14-15) and Summer 1987 (pp. 31-32).

2. Walter Hooper, "Reflections of an Editor," *CSL: The Bulletin of the New York C. S. Lewis Society* (August 1977), 1-2.

3. The following is the text of Warren Lewis's letter to me:
The Kilns, Kiln Lane
Headington Quarry, Oxford
24th April 1964

Dear Mrs. Lindskoog,
I am most grateful to you for your kindness in sending me the copy of my brother's letter to you, which is interesting, and which I think I can use.
Now as regards your questions:—

(1) I have no recordings of his voice, and so far as I know, the only people who might have them would be the British Broadcasting Co. I believe when one broadcasts for them, a tape is made of the broadcast.
(2) My brother had been ailing for some considerable time with a kidney complaint, but what actually finished him was a stroke.
(3) He married in 1956, but I don't know the exact date. His wife died on 13th June [sic] 1960.
(4) There are two stepsons who may I think be described as semi-adult. The elder is 20 and the other one over 18.
There is nothing private about these facts.
With all good wishes, & thanks.

Yours sincerely,
W. H. Lewis

4. Letter from W. H. Lewis to me, 3 February 1967.
5. Letter from W. H. Lewis to me, 13 July 1967.
6. The speech was given on 16 August 1975 at Mythcon VI, held on the campus of Scripps College at Claremont, California.
7. The London speech was presented on 2 March 1977 at Church House, Westminster, at an event organized by Nigel Sustins upon the occasion

of publication of *The Dark Tower*. About 150 people attended, and speakers included Walter Hooper, Owen Barfield, Roger Lancelyn Green, Priscilla Tolkien, and actor Robert Eddison. In Mary Kirkpatrick's report "A Lewis Evening in London," (page 1 of the April 1977 issue of *CSL*), she noted that Hooper said he saved "a small mountain" of papers from the bonfire. The New York speech was presented on 13 August 1977 at a C. S. Lewis Weekend on the campus of Albertus Magnus College in New Haven, Connecticut. It was then published as "Reflections of an Editor" in the August 1977 issue of *CSL*.

8. Letter from Leonard Miller to me, 26 October 1977.
9. In a letter to me postmarked 9 December 1977 and written from 5 The Square, Churchill, OXON, F. W. Paxford said "In all my failings, one is that I am much too independent. So it cuts out begging the Major, much less Walter Hooper anyway. To me, the whole thing sounds phoney and I cannot see the Major burning any papers that were important."
10. *Christianity & Literature*, Winter 1979, 12-13.
11. The following personal letter from Dr. Walter R. Hearn to me on 10 March 1988 offers information about Anthony Marchington's bonfire letter and his subsequent career.

"I have read the letter by Anthony F. Marchington published in *Christianity & Literature*, Vol. 28 (2) Winter 1979, pp. 12-13, concerning chemical examination of residues from bonfires. In your book manuscript you add that the Marchington letter was on official stationery of the Physical Chemistry Laboratory of Oxford University. Although the letter is in the form of a report from that laboratory, I think it has all the earmarks of a practical joke.

"Without personal experience in forensic or archaeological chemistry, I can imagine that spectroscopy or other techniques might enable one to distinguish ashes from certain kinds of incompletely combusted materials. The claims of the letter and the wording of the accompanying footnotes, however, leave me totally skeptical about this report's authenticity. The idea that 'computer structural data analysis of particle sizes' could yield 'both date and average temperature' of a bonfire sounds preposterous to me. Reporting that the date of burning of the Coventry Cathedral bible was pinpointed to within six months by such a technique I suspect is the author's way of making sure that only the most gullible readers will be taken in by his hoax.

"At any rate, no mention of such methods is made in two symposia on the chemistry of archaeology published by the American Chemical Society in 1973 and 1977, or in a standard work by Zvi Goffer, *Archaeological Chemistry: A Sourcebook on the Applications of Chemistry to Archaeology* (New York: John Wiley and Sons, 1980). There is no record in *Chemical Abstracts* that the promised paper by "Marchington, Pigot-Churchhouse, and Wizard" was ever published.

"Anthony F. Marchington is indeed a real person with training in physical chemistry and computers, however. He has published a number of technical papers, first with William Graham Richards and coworkers at the Physical Chemistry Laboratory at Oxford. He began with a study of the inductive effect in molecules and ions, using computer calculations. He used computer graphics of visualization of three-dimensional structures in studies of enzyme-substrate interactions at Oxford and then for the design of new fungicides at the Jealotts Hill Research Station of Imperial Chemical Industries Plant Protection Division in Bracknell/Berkshire, UK RG12 6EY. His name appears on a British patent for such compounds (assigned to ICI), and in 1984 he published a review of computer graphics in the design of triazole fungicides."

Dr. Hearn has a bachelor's degree in chemistry from Rice University and a Ph.D. in biochemistry from the University of Illinois. He served on the biochemistry faculties of the medical schools of Yale and Baylor Universities and then of Iowa State University, which he left in 1972. He now lives in Berkeley, California and edits the Newsletter of the American Scientific Affiliation.

12. The editor of *Christianity & Literature* gave me a clear photocopy of Marchington's bonfire letter. I have on hand samples of Hooper's typing from 1973, 1979, and 1980 (about twenty pages).

SEEING THROUGH "THROUGH JOY AND BEYOND"

Anthony Marchington, the Lewis bonfire jokester, entered Brasenose College in 1973. When he wrote his letter about soot analysis for *Christianity & Literature* he was still an anonymous university student. He had been living with his close friend Walter Hooper near the Eagle and Child (Bird and Baby) pub in Oxford, in a tiny upstairs apartment at 19 Beaumont Street.[1] Marchington studied science, and Hooper managed the C. S. Lewis estate.

But Marchington and Hooper collaborated on projects of mutual interest. One of them was probably the article that Hooper coauthored with a friend and published in *Oxford* magazine under the single pen name Walter Churchington. It defended the tradition of excluding females from the all male colleges.[2]

The collaboration that would eventually make Marchington a public figure in the United States began with a telephone call back in September 1977. Walter Hooper's Illinois friend Bob O'Donnell called Hooper with a request. He wanted permission from the C. S. Lewis estate to make a C. S. Lewis film.[3] O'Donnell was not the first or last to have that wish; but he had the inside track and permission was granted.[4]

O'Donnell was the actor who played the unscrupulous Commander in "The Gospel Blimp," a widely circulated rental film based upon Joseph Bayly's satirical book with that name.[5] The long-term popularity of that film in evangelical churches has been impressive. It seemed obvious that a film about C. S. Lewis might appeal to that market as well as to Episcopal churches and to colleges and seminaries; and it might be aired on television.

A bold plan was hatched by O'Donnell and Hooper. O'Donnell would serve as producer and director; and Hooper would serve as author and on-camera narrator.[6] Peter Ustinov would be hired to read all the passages of literature used in the film. As Hooper tells it, he immediately consulted Marchington about the project and included him as coauthor of the script and as assistant producer.[7]

In March of 1978, Bob O'Donnell arrived to arrange for a summer film crew. In May a bit of preliminary filming was done. In June, Hooper and Marchington completed the script, and in July they began full-time filming. In August Bob O'Donnell and some helpers flew to Palermo, Sicily, to meet Peter Ustinov for his readings. In the fall the film was edited in Illinois, and major publicity was being prepared by the distributor, Gospel Films.

Anachronistic as it may seem, in the 8 July 1983 issue of *National Review*, H. N. Kelley devoted almost a page[8] to publicity for the four-year-old film, beginning, "Bob O'Donnell is a man who believes in putting his money where his heart is. He sank five years [sic] and vast quantities of his own money into producing a documentary film on the life of C. S. Lewis, entitled *Through Joy and Beyond*, simply, he says, 'to help get people interested in reading Lewis.'" Kelley ended his article with the claim that when Walter Hooper toured the United States to answer questions about C. S. Lewis, he found to his surprise that his heavily evangelical audiences were not much interested in Lewis's life and beliefs, but wanted to know instead about his smoking and drinking habits.

Kelley was wrong about the evangelical questions, and he was wrong about the year of the tour, which he placed in 1982. But he was right that there was a tour. The film premiered in "A Visit with C. S. Lewis" seminars in twenty cities around the United States in February, March, and April of 1979. Full-page ads appeared in magazines, handsome full-color brochures were sent to homes, large full-color posters were mailed out, and a special half-hour preview film was given to television broadcasters. Newspapers were contacted personally and urged to interview Hooper. In the publicity and in the film itself, Anthony Marchington's name was placed right next to Walter Hooper's as coauthor.

The entire film turned out to be two-and-a-half hours long and comes in three reels, only two of which were used in the seminars. The first reel is called "The Formative Years," and in it Hooper covers Lewis's childhood and youth until shortly after the First World War. The second reel is called "The Informed Years," and in it Hooper covers the rest of Lewis's life. The third reel is called "Jack Remembered" and features Hooper introducing a few of Lewis's many friends—Dr. Robert Havard, John and Priscilla Tolkien, Pauline Baynes, and Owen Barfield. And Anthony Marchington!

Viewers all over the United States have now met Anthony Marchington at the end of "Jack Remembered."
He appears as the president of a small men's dining club
in the Oxford tradition (it is not clear whether this is a
real club or a fictitious one), where the members wear
tuxedos and enjoy formal British dining. Hooper explains
that the men have enjoyed a seven-course dinner with
dessert and "fruits as to the season." Then Anthony Marchington introduces the after-dinner speaker, Martin
Moynihan, who reminisces briefly about C. S. Lewis.

During the speech, the young men puff on big cigars
and sip port wine. Anthony Marchington sits at the
speaker's left, puffing dutifully. He looks as if he is in his
midtwenties, with rather long, thick, curly brown hair
which he tugs on at times. He tends to slump at the
table. To his left is Walter Hooper, in his late forties,
leaning on the table with an intensely appreciative expres-
sion, also making a show of his cigar. Lingering close-ups
of some of the other club members, apparently personal
friends of Marchington, give the impression that they
were more interested in the film than in the speech. One
of them has a face twinkling with silent laughter. Could
one of these young men be Marchington's "academic
supervisor Dr. Stephen C. F. Moore"? The men puff and
sip with an air of bemused bonhomie.

When Sheldon Vanauken—author of *A Severe Mercy*,
personal friend of C. S. Lewis, and lover of Oxford—
heard about this scene, he wrote to me, "It sounds very
odd indeed to me. I myself belonged to a dining club at
Oxford. One of the first things I learned there was that
one never, never smokes with port wine. Cigars would
kill the port. With the fruit, one drinks port. *Then* coffee
and cigars or pipes."

Perhaps the cigars were only symbolic and the dinner a fiction anyway. It was a rather curious way to end the film, but an unexpected opportunity to see and hear the author of the Lewis Bonfire letter, coauthor of the film itself, and—just possibly— the author or coauthor of *The Dark Tower*.

Anyone who wants to see Anthony Marchington without watching the film can find his picture on page 79 of the book made from the film, Walter Hooper's *Through Joy and Beyond* (Macmillan, 1982). Marchington was named as coauthor on the front of the book until the last minute, when his name was removed from the cover.[9] Two years after publication of the book, Walter Hooper was summoned to Rome so that Pope John Paul II could talk with him about C. S. Lewis, and he had his photo taken while presenting a copy of *Through Joy and Beyond* to the Pope.[10]

Although most of the film *Through Joy and Beyond* is accurate and interesting, if not highly professional, there are a few minor errors and some significant distortions in it.

Minor errors include using what Lewis said about Malvern to describe Surrey; placing Lewis's famous atheism letter after instead of before his service in the trenches of World War I; making Warren Lewis into a Major before World War II; the idea that Lewis enjoyed his heavy burden of correspondence; the idea that Lewis had to constantly deny to readers that he had ever traveled in outer space; the idea that children's literature is the particular branch of literature in which few authors attain more than a transitory or esoteric fame; and the idea that Lewis could get from Magdalen College to his home at Headington Quarry by walking around Addison's Walk (a one-mile circular walk at Magdalen College). These suggestions are surprising, but they can be shrugged off as the result of hasty production.

More deliberate was the substitution of a hydrangea bush for the currant bush that changed Lewis's life when he was a young child. That is where he first met the spiritual longing that he called Joy, which shaped his life.[11] Lewis wrote near the beginning of his autobiography *Surprised by Joy*, "As I stood by a flowering currant bush on a summer day . . ." Lewis's words are changed in the film, and viewers see a hydrangea bush in bloom. What came through the bush changed Lewis for life and eventually led him to Christianity; that point is clear. But the tone is different. It is as if an oak tree took the place of a pine tree, a detail that matters to some people and to others not at all. It did matter to C. S. Lewis, of course. He was attuned to nature.

Next, a big heavy hydrangea blossom was stuck into the film version of a miniature garden that gave C. S. Lewis his lifetime love of nature. A red rose, other oversize vegetation, and some knickknacks completed the film garden; it lacked the delicacy and simplicity of the original garden Lewis described. This lapse is a matter of scale and style.

Far more prominent is the puzzling choirboy sequence in the film. Of all the interesting people and places that could have been included and weren't, seven minutes (almost one-eighth of "The Informed Years") is devoted to a boys' choir singing in the chapel at Magdalen College, Oxford. Hooper has described the music as "ravishingly beautiful," and gives the impression that as soon as Lewis came to believe in God he started attending Evensong and listening to the boys' choir. But Lewis said that he attended morning rather than evening chapel;

and he made it clear that whenever he went to worship, he did not enjoy church music. The film indicates the opposite. I have noticed that some viewers find the lingering close-up of one boy's face, then another's, irritating and distracting.[12] Too close, some viewers feel, for comfort. Too long for comfort, others complain. I believe C. S. Lewis would agree on both counts. Any hint of aesthetic pederasty is out of place in a C. S. Lewis film.[13] Is there a hint? I believe so. The result is certainly inappropriate.

Far more complex is the doubtful claim in the film about a major part of Lewis's personal life. Hooper tells the charming story about how C. S. Lewis and his army friend Paddy Moore pledged to each other that if only one of them returned from France alive, he would care for his friend's parent for life. That is supposed to account for Lewis living with the ignorant, self-centered, overbearing Mrs. Moore for over thirty years.

The fact is that such a two-way promise would not have made any sense. C. S. Lewis's father Albert, a successful Belfast attorney, was a widower with two sons and many other relatives. He was moody, eccentric, and set in his ways. He certainly would not have wanted a young stranger with his dependent mother and little sister in tow, "rescuing" him. The idea is ridiculous, and C. S. Lewis would not have entertained it for a moment.[14] Furthermore, there was no particular affinity between Lewis and Paddy Moore in the first place; they paired off simply because they were put together alphabetically.[15] They were not really close friends.

Sixty years before Walter Hooper told about the two-way promise, Mrs. Moore claimed that there was a one-way promise. She wrote to C. S. Lewis's father Albert and told him that his son had promised Paddy that he would care for her after the war if Paddy didn't come back. Albert thought that was not an adequate explanation for what was going on. He was right.

In retrospect, two historical facts seem to undermine Mrs. Moore's story of a unilateral promise. First, according to both C. S. Lewis and Warren Lewis, she often spoke untruth. Second, C. S. Lewis never told anyone of such a promise. It would have cleared the air, but Lewis never made that claim. Only once did Warren Lewis dare to bring up the question of why C. S. Lewis lived with Mrs. Moore, and he was told to mind his own business.[16]

Furthermore, if Lewis really had made a unilateral promise to take Paddy's place for Mrs. Moore, that would hardly have obligated him to live under her domestic tyranny until she died. No one thinks that Paddy Moore would have lived on with her as an adult. He did not get along with her.[17]

In fact, Albert Lewis called his son Jack's relationship to Mrs. Moore an affair, and he was intensely upset about Jack living with a woman old enough to be his mother. C. S. Lewis's behavior completely confirmed his father's impression. In his autobiography, C. S. Lewis left Mrs. Moore out entirely. He simply confessed that at the end of the First World War there came a huge, complex episode in his life that he could not divulge; he greatly regretted it, and it taught him to avoid unbridled emotionalism the rest of his life.

It certainly looks as if Lewis's submission to Mrs. Moore and his avoidance of romantic involvement so long as she lived was his form of extreme *noblesse oblige* after a period of youthful indiscretion. It was no dedication to the memory of Paddy Moore that bound C. S. Lewis to the chaos of Mrs. Moore for over thirty years, and

Hooper's attempts to portray her as a pleasant companion don't fit the facts.

The second major misrepresentation in the film is about the other woman who lived with C. S. Lewis, his wife Joy Davidman. She receives only two minutes of attention. "It was in 1952 that Lewis first met Joy Davidman. She had ambitions as a writer and had long admired Lewis." In fact, she had more than ambitions as a writer; she had prizes and books to her credit. The film goes on to say that she had left her husband and two young sons behind in New York while she spent a year in England. Upon her return, the film says, her husband divorced her. More accurately, she left her husband and sons in the care of her cousin while she stayed in England for six months. C. S. Lewis advised her to divorce her husband, who was unfaithful, alcoholic, and sometimes violent. She delayed filing for divorce when she got home, and her husband did the filing so he could marry his mistress, her cousin, as soon as possible.

The film makes a big point of the fact that although Lewis married Joy Davidman, he never considered consummating the marriage. There is so much evidence to the contrary that this opinion is untenable. Both C. S. Lewis and Joy Lewis indicated to friends that the marriage was consummated, and one of the stepsons claims that he accidentally witnessed the fact once by walking in on them.[18]

The treatment of Warren Lewis in this film is also unbalanced. "As for Warnie, he was fast sliding into serious alcoholism." It is true that Major Lewis was a functioning alcoholic most of his adult life. But so little is said about him in the film that the additional statement "Much of the time Warnie was away—drunk—in Ireland" tips the scales too far. Not a word is said about Warren being a devout Christian, a successful author on his own, and C. S. Lewis's personal secretary.

Hooper tells about his own relationship to C. S. Lewis near the end of "The Informed Years": "In fact, I first met him early in 1963; and as we grew more intimate he asked me to become his companion-secretary and I moved here to the Kilns." But according to William Griffin's biography *C. S. Lewis: A Dramatic Life*, Walter Hooper first met C. S. Lewis on 7 June 1963. And whatever Hooper means by "intimate," Leonard and Mollie Miller claimed that Hooper had a room in Oxford and never really moved in. [19]

The droll anecdotes that Hooper tells about himself and C. S. Lewis in the film take up about three minutes and give an excellent example of his skill as a winsome storyteller. He is a talented raconteur who radiates humility and cheer.

In the summer of 1987 Walter Hooper addressed a C. S. Lewis and G. K. Chesterton conference in Seattle, Washington, and received a standing ovation. A member of the audience noted, "My two friends regard him as a kind of Tartuffe. . . . I don't know what to think myself, and it's a mercy I'm not likely to be called on to make a judgment. His style as a speaker is enormously effective: self-deprecating, soft-spoken, with a masterly light touch."[20]

Walter Hooper exercised this storytelling skill before large audiences in his 1979 tour. When he appeared on stage at the Pasadena Civic Auditorium in California, his habits of thinking and speaking gave people the impression that he was a stranger here. He referred to his audience as "you Americans," acted bewildered by American geography, and marveled at the American love for gadgets. No one would have guessed that he was thirty-two years old when he first visited England; most people assumed he was born there.

Hooper began to seem English long before the film. In 1973 author Robert Ellwood, a professor of religion at the University of Southern California and an ordained Episcopal priest, was in England on a sabbatical and went with his wife Gracia Fay Ellwood, an author interested in Tolkien and Lewis, to meet the forty-two-year-old Walter Hooper. As Gracia Fay Ellwood told me later, Hooper seemed uninformed about American education; therefore, Robert Ellwood took much time to explain the American school system to him. Hooper seemed to the Ellwoods to be interested and grateful. After they got back to the United States, they learned to their surprise that Hooper was really as American as they were.

It is possible that Hooper pretended to be English in order to be more like Lewis; and it is possible that he denies Lewis's sexual intercourse with women in order to qualify Lewis for sainthood.

Furthermore, Hooper may deny that Lewis had wandering thoughts during church in order to please himself and other clerics. That happened in the film *Through Joy and Beyond* when Hooper altered slightly the origin of Lewis's *Screwtape Letters*. In the film, Hooper stands in Lewis's parish churchyard and declares, "It was here, following an 8 a.m. Communion service, that the book which brought him international fame was conceived. Writing to his brother Warren, he said, 'After the service was over, I was struck by an idea for a book.'"

But Lewis did not conceive of the book in the churchyard after the 8 a.m. service. In his letter to Warren he makes that quite clear. On that fateful Sunday he had gone to midday church service, and he wrote to Warren, "Before the service was over—one could wish these things came more seasonably—I was struck by an idea for a book."[21]

It is a minor change, but minor changes add up.

The Screwtape Letters received much attention in *Through Joy and Beyond* and the special edition produced by Lord and King was displayed in the film itself, then sold in the lobby after the seminar. An order blank for the Lord and King edition accompanies the film when it is rented. And that edition has been distributed nationwide by Spire Books to this day. But some of it is not what Lewis really wrote. That is the subject of chapter 5.

Chapter 4, Notes

1. On 26 April 1978, Walter Hooper wrote in his Editor's Note that he shared his home with Anthony Marchington and that Marchington was his helper (C. S. Lewis, *They Stand Together* [New York: Macmillan, 1979], 45).

2. Sheldon Vanauken read the article and wrote to Churchington in agreement. To his surprise, he got a letter from Walter Hooper revealing that he and a friend had published it under this pseudonym.

3. Hooper's Introduction to *Through Joy and Beyond* (New York: Macmillan, 1982), xi.

4. In contrast, when an admirer of Clyde S. Kilby sought permission to make a film of Dr. Kilby and the C. S. Lewis collection at Wheaton College (now called the Wade Center), the C. S. Lewis estate denied permission for filming of Lewis materials and the film was canceled.

5. On 1 February 1978, Joseph Bayly remarked in regard to some behind-the-scenes business in Lewis affairs, "In this as in so many things, I feel that the cause of Christ really suffers because people are unwilling to 'stick their necks out'."

6. *Through Joy and Beyond*, xi.

7. Ibid., xii.

8. H. N. Kelley, "The Lewis Tapes," *National Review*, 8 July 1983, 834, 836. Kelley, referring to Hooper's centrality in the film, comments, "Father Hooper, of course, knows Lewis as no one else possibly could. He was his secretary, lived with him, attended the famous Inklings meetings with him, talked endlessly with Lewis as he reminisced in his final days."

9. The original cover design for *Through Joy and Beyond* was pictured on the inside of the front cover of the Advent issue of *The Anglican Digest* in 1982.

10. Walter Hooper's account of his meeting with Pope John Paul II appeared in the February 1987 issue of *The Chesterton Review*, 132-39. Hooper discovered that Pope John Paul II was very much like C. S. Lewis. Talking

to the Pope was like talking to Lewis. First, the Pope asked Hooper, "Do you still love your old friend, C. S. Lewis?" Soon the Pope told Hooper that editing Lewis's books was Hooper's *apostolate* (mission). "Our Wal-ter Hoo-per— you are doing very good WORK!"

At the beginning and end of the conversation, Hooper knelt and kissed the Pope's ring. Both times, a miracle took place, although bystanders would not realize it. The first miracle was dramatically obvious to both Hooper and the Pope, and bound them in a mystical way. The Pope whispered to Hooper, "I understand." The second miracle, in which Hooper gladly took into himself some intense suffering of the Pope's, was known to Hooper alone—and to God—until Hooper decided to tell all his readers.

In Hooper's account, it seems that Pope John Paul II has endorsed Hooper's career in Lewis affairs, and it seems that God has endorsed the Pope's endorsement—with miracles before and after. Needless to say, questioning the accuracy of Hooper's account would seem indelicate at best, and sacrilegious at worst. It puts doubters in an awkward position.

11. In Warren Lewis's diary entry on 21 March 1967 (Warren Lewis, *Brothers and Friends* [San Francisco: Harper & Row, 1982], 272), he explained what flowering currants meant. "The flowering currant is now out in several places, and this is always one of the highlights of my year. Enjoyment of it and the wallflower are the earliest aesthetic experiences of my life—dating back to long before we left Dundela Villas. I can still remember the thrill of joy with which I used to greet the arrival of both, a thrill which one never experiences once childhood is past; and which is perhaps the purest one ever receives. Is it I wonder wholly fanciful to think that this thrill is a dim recollection of having just *come* from a better world?"

12. When I saw the film in Pasadena in 1979 and in Costa Mesa in 1987, I heard several complaints that the choirboy sequences were too close or too long for comfort.

13. "People commonly talk as if every other evil were more tolerable than this [pederasty]. But why? Because those of us who do not share the vice feel for it a certain nausea, as we do, say, for necrophily?" C. S. Lewis, *Surprised by Joy* (London: Geoffrey Bles, 1955), 107.

14. On 30 July 1966, Major Warren Lewis received a letter from his cousin Ruth Hamilton Parker in response to his 1966 publication of C. S. Lewis letters. She reflected upon Albert Lewis and her parents discussing the exasperating misfortune of Mrs. Moore's entry into C. S. Lewis's life: "Dear me, how they talked and talked. Uncle A. wanted to know if Jack had been killed would *he* have been adopted by the Moore boy." *Brothers and Friends*, 264.

15. Warren Lewis, *Letters of C. S. Lewis* (New York: Harcourt, Brace & World, 1966), 8.

16. Roger Lancelyn Green and Walter Hooper, *C. S. Lewis: A Biography* (London: Collins, 1974), 66.

17. *Brothers and Friends*, 233.

18. Douglas Gresham, "C. S. Lewis: Memories of a Compassionate Man." The Ninth Annual Wade Lecture, delivered at Wheaton College on 4

November 1983. Available as cassette tape 8406 0107.

19. Stated by Leonard Miller in letters to me dated 26 January 1978 and 15 February 1978: "Hooper never lived at the Kilns whilst C. S. Lewis was alive. During that period he lodged somewhere in Oxford. But I don't know where."

20. A letter to me from an ex-student and casual friend of C. S. Lewis, dated 20 July 1987.

21. *The Screwtape Letters* (W. Chicago, Ill.: Lord and King Associates, 1976), 7.

5.

STRANGE VISIONS AND REVISIONS

I̤t used to be said that there were two kinds of Lewis readers: those who read *The Screwtape Letters* and stop, and those who read *The Screwtape Letters* and continue. That is how very popular Lewis's popular psychology was in this 1942 book that eventually put C. S. Lewis on the cover of *Time* magazine[1]

"C. S. Lewis's *The Screwtape Letters* is one of the great incongruities of modern literature: a moral tract which was also a sensational bestseller. Cast in the form of a one-way correspondence—the helpful letters of an other-worldly-wise demon to his nephew, an apprentice in the business—it has a rich and civilized wit." That begins the preface to the 1963 Time Reading Program edition. Screwtape was twenty-one years old, and as Phyllis McGinley observed in her fine introduction, a classic:

"something that survives its own generation and continues to enchant and seduce."

Some recent editions have included Lewis's 1959 *Saturday Evening Post* essay "Screwtape Proposes a Toast," his only other writing about this literally infernal bureaucrat and the lowerarchy he is a part of. All the various editions sell handsomely.

In 1976 Walter Hooper and Bob O'Donnell of Lord and King Associates in Illinois brought out an unusual new edition of *The Screwtape Letters*.[2] The introduction to this new edition states mysteriously that "some papers" recently "came to light" which tell how Lewis got the idea for the book. As a matter of fact, Warren Lewis willed all his letters and papers to the Marion E. Wade Center for research purposes, and the Wade Center gave copies to the Bodleian Library in Oxford. That is how the "papers came to light"—as an intentional gift to the public from Major Lewis. It often happens that simple facts seem mysterious or portentous because they are dramatized; but sometimes very mysterious subjects indeed are lightly brushed aside.

Although Hooper introduces *The Screwtape Letters* with scholarly flourish, he starts right out with a peculiar inaccuracy that makes a muddle of when Lewis got his inspiration for the book. In reality Lewis started a letter to his brother on 20 July 1940, got his inspiration in church on July 21, and then completed the letter to his brother. Hooper claims that Lewis got the inspiration on July 14—when in fact Lewis was in bed with the flu—and wrote to his brother about it on July 20. The fact that Hooper blocks publication of Lewis's letter, as well as misrepresenting what it says, perpetuates Hooper's distortion of the historic event.[3]

In itself the misreading of C. S. Lewis's letter to his brother is no harmful error, although it seems a shame that the reading public has no access to that especially long and interesting letter except for a brief excerpt.[4] But unfortunately the initial error sets the tone for the entire edition. And this edition came out in six different forms at once: (1) a $40 autographed book (not autographed by Lewis, of course), advertised as bound in real leather; (2) a $15 hardback book; (3) a large $5 paperback book; (4) a small $1.75 paperback book (now $3.50 from Spire); (5) a $25 phonograph album; (6) a $50 album of six cassette tapes.

The surprising thing about all six products is that they appear to offer *The Screwtape Letters* as Lewis wrote it. There is no warning on the cover or title page that some of Lewis's words (and meanings) have been changed. In the small paperback, the most popular of the items, readers have to read more than eight solid pages of introduction before they get to the key fact buried in the middle of a paragraph on the ninth page—the fact that Walter Hooper and Owen Barfield have allowed "slight alterations" in the text.

Few readers will take time to read the entire introduction in the first place, and those who do won't know the audacity of the changes that have been made. To add to the confusion, in 1982 Macmillan brought out a new edition of *The Screwtape Letters* that states boldly on the cover "Revised Edition"—and it is not revised at all. It is in Lewis's own words throughout.

The most wrenching change in the Lord and King version is that the Second World War story is moved from England to the United States, bombing and all. The British Museum is changed to the Metropolitan Library.[5] German leaders are changed to Enemy leaders;[6] but because in this book Enemy stands for God, German leaders have been turned into God's leaders.

In Letter Eleven the attitude of the English to humor is changed to the attitude of "the modern generation." The verb "twits" is changed to "kids," and "a comical fellow" is changed to "a comic." "English" seriousness about humor is changed to "modern" seriousness about humor—a purported trend that Lewis himself never noted. Television is brought in.

In Letter Sixteen Lewis's reference to Jacques Maritain is replaced by a reference to none other than C. S. Lewis himself. The French Roman Catholic philosopher might be surprised to see himself turned into Lewis, but surely Lewis's amazement would be greater. Popping C. S. Lewis into his own book is a bit of drollery that reminds me of his uncomfortable presence in *The Dark Tower*.

In Letter Seventeen the English are changed into Americans, thus indicating that Lewis thought Americans were especially given to the theory that vigorous athletic activity contributes to chastity.

These changes in the text were copyrighted in 1976 by Lord and King Associates, and "no part thereof may be reproduced or transmitted in any form, or by any means, electronic or mechanical." Thank goodness.

Hooper ended his nine-page introduction to this edition of *The Screwtape Letters* with a humble anecdote about finding C. S. Lewis up to his elbows in soap suds after dinner on 7 August 1963—when in fact Lewis was an invalid who had just got home from the hospital.[7] On August 10 Lewis was still too weak to write a letter or to receive guests. It is hard to imagine Lewis washing the supper dishes in such condition and laughing to Hooper, "If ever you tell what it is like in this house, you must say that not only are the servants soft underfoot but *invisible* as well."

Actually, Lewis had used the term "soft underfoot" in *The Screwtape Letters*, and it referred to the soft path that leads to destruction.[8] It seems highly unlikely that wordmaster Lewis would have described people (invisible or not) as soft underfoot, like carpeting. And since he had a gardener, housekeeper, and live-in nurse at that time, the claim to no servants doesn't make much sense. But many people find the account charming. Who would not like to be part of that happy camaraderie that Hooper describes?

The Screwtape Letters was only the ninth of eighteen books by C. S. Lewis that have introductions by Walter Hooper at this counting. Most of these introductions have a personal touch. Here is the tally at present, with brief excerpts to illustrate the warm personal style and sense of intimacy with C. S. Lewis that Hooper often expresses:

1. *Poems*, 1964. Seven-page introduction. "When I was his secretary, he sometimes used to dictate poems. Even after he thought one was completed, he might suggest a change here. Then a change there."

2. *Studies in Medieval and Renaissance Literature*, 1966. Four-page introduction. "'Yes,' I said, 'Would you like them?' [Lewis wished for some of Hooper's books.] There was a very long pause. 'After what I have just said,' he fumbled, 'would you—*could* you part with them?'"

3. *Of Other Worlds*, 1966. Six-page introduction. "At that moment I was pouring tea into a very large Cornish-ware cup."

4. *Christian Reflections*, 1967. Eight-page introduction. "I remember one very warm day when Lewis and I were reading in his study that I remarked, rather too loudly,

'Whew! It's hot as hell!'"

5. *Narrative Poems*, 1969. Eight-page introduction. "As far as I know, the only manuscript of *Dymer* to escape being burnt consists of eighty-six pages of rough draft . . . which were written in one of Lewis's notebooks now in my possession."

6. *Selected Literary Essays*, 1969. Fourteen-page introduction. "I inherited from Lewis's library most of the texts he used while reading Greats and English."

7. *God in the Dock*, 1970. Eleven-page introduction. "One day he and I were wondering what would happen if a group of friendly and inquisitive Martians suddenly appeared in the middle of Oxford. . . . On the whole, we doubted whether the Martians would take back to their world much that is worth having."

8. *Fernseeds and Elephants*, 1975. Three-page introduction. "Professor Tolkien once teased me about C. S. Lewis. . . . He had in his hands at that moment the seventh volume of Lewis's writings which I had edited."

9. *The Screwtape Letters*, 1976. Nine-page introduction. "When invited to write a preface for this special edition of *Screwtape* my mind was carried back to the inexpressibly happy period that I spent as C. S. Lewis's secretary."

10. *The Dark Tower*, 1977. Eleven-page introduction. "There were so many that it took all my strength and energy to carry them back to Keble College. That evening, while glancing through them, I came across a manuscript which excited me very much."

11. *They Stand Together*, 1979. Thirty-seven-page introduction. "Meanwhile, Lewis and I became more intimate, and finally he asked me to become his companion-secretary and I moved into his house."

12. *The Weight of Glory*, 1980. Sixteen-page introduction. "'Informer!' roared Lewis. 'I have what no friend ever had before. I have a private traitor, my very own personal Benedict Arnold. Repent before it is too late!' I loved all the rough and tumble of this, and I fancy I pulled his leg about as often as he pulled mine."

13. *Mere Christianity*, 1981. Twenty-eight-page introduction. "I learned of it when I became, near the end of his life, Lewis's private secretary."

14. *On Stories and Other Essays*, 1982. Thirteen-page introduction. "Best of all was the day when Mr. Fleming and I sat in the drawing room of the Athenaeum Club in London [an exclusive club that Walter Hooper has joined], reading the original manuscript—which Lewis had given him."

15. *The Business of Heaven*, 1984. Seven-page introduction. "You will find that I hammer away pretty hard with passages about morality." [Hooper means that in choosing Lewis selections he favors those that stress morality.]

16. *Spirits in Bondage*, 1984. Twenty-eight-page introduction. "It was while I was his private secretary in the last months of his life that the curtain was lifted just a little."

17. *Boxen*, 1984. Fifteen-page introduction. "I first read the Boxen 'novels' during that part of 1963 when I was Jack's secretary and living in his home in Oxford. When he discovered how charmed I was . . ."

18. *Present Concerns*, 1987. Five-page introduction. "'Who is Elizabeth Taylor?' asked C. S. Lewis. He and I were talking about the difference between 'prettiness' and 'beauty,' and I suggested that Miss Taylor was a great beauty. 'If you read the newspapers,' I said to Lewis, 'you would know who she is.'"

Altogether, these eighteen C. S. Lewis books contain 230 pages by Walter Hooper, enough to fill a separate book. Surely C. S. Lewis would be amazed to see so much by another person between his own book covers, especially if Lewis did not consider Hooper his secretary after all.

Not surprisingly, production of Lewis books has come to the point where Hooper has seen fit to place his own dedication at the front of a recent one, *On Stories and Other Essays*:

> To Priscilla Collins this collection of Lewis essays is dedicated by the Trustees of his Estate in token of their respect and admiration, and in gratitude for the unfailing support they have enjoyed from her in the endeavor to fulfill that trust in a manner worthy of its object.
>
> Owen Barfield
> Walter Hooper

These three people—Priscilla Collins, Owen Barfield, and Walter Hooper—have been the major official decision-makers in C. S. Lewis affairs since his death. Lady Priscilla Collins is the primary publisher of C. S. Lewis's writings. Collins is a large publisher that bought the Geoffrey Bles company and thus acquired most of Lewis's books.

Although most good and bad decisions about Lewis books have been made or delegated by these three people, the rights to some of Lewis's books have been elsewhere. And although most footnotes added to Lewis books are by Walter Hooper (and most of these are competent and dependable), that is not always the case.

No other book by C. S. Lewis is edited so strangely as *The Pilgrim's Regress*, his book that needs notes most of all. U. S. rights are owned by the William B. Eerdmans

Publishing Company, which sold reprint rights for an annotated mass paperback edition to Bantam Books. Since 1981 Bantam has been selling Lewis's allegory with explanatory notes by an unidentified Dr. John C. Traupman who, according to the title page, supplies translations and data.

Of all the hundreds of things that readers need to be told in order to get more out of *The Pilgrim's Regress* (because, as Lewis was quick to admit, he wrote it for a small circle of "highbrow" readers), Dr. Traupman chose thirty phrases to identify in his endnotes. Of those thirty, his explanation of nineteen of the phrases is "Source unknown."

For "The fool hath said . . . [in his heart there is no God]" Traupman's note is simply "Source unknown." So they go. But for "The sin of Adam" he tried to be more helpful. He told the readers, "Source unknown. Lord Byron refers to an 'Ada.'"

Some of the harshest words Lewis ever penned were about publishers. But ridiculous additions to his books certainly would not irritate him so much as changes in what he wrote.

Some readers become disturbed if they feel that Lewis's writing has been altered without warning to the reader. Of course, anyone who hears about the changes in *The Screwtape Letters* can check the altered version with the original version to correct it. But, in contrast, few people can get to a library that has Lewis's original published version of "The Humanitarian Theory of Punishment" in the Australian publication *Twentieth Century*. As the essay appears in *God in the Dock*, the final paragraph has been left off. There Lewis stated that in 1948 he couldn't get the essay published in England:

One last word. You may ask why I send this to an Australian periodical. The reason is simple and perhaps worth recording: I can get no hearing for it in England.

This bit of social history is particularly interesting now that Lewis's views on the topic finally can get a hearing because crime experts are beginning to accept his ideas forty years later.

But far more disturbing are cases like *The Dark Tower* where there has been no previous publication at all, and so there is no possible way to check. In the collection called *The Dark Tower* there is one short story that has never been published before, in addition to the unfinished novel. It is "The Man Born Blind." The writing is so flat, talky, and amateurish that it seems impossible that Lewis could have written it.

Hooper says that he found this story in Lewis's handwriting in notebooks that Warren Lewis gave to him, and that Lewis had obviously worked on the story years after he first penned it.[9] If that account is true, it raises important questions about the contents of those notebooks and what was wrong with Lewis. But if the account is false, it raises the question of why the writer who was imitating Lewis did such a poor job. The story simply does not sound like Lewis at all.

Here is a sample of the dialogue:

"The sun makes it . . . hot?" said Robin tentatively.

"What are you talking about?" said Mary, suddenly turning around.

"I mean," said Robin, ". . . well, look here, Mary. There's a thing I've been meaning to ask you ever

since I came back from the nursing home. I know
it'll sound silly to you . . ."

From the useless adverb *tentatively* to the awkward use
of *it'll*, there are several flaws in this brief passage that
make it unworthy of Lewis or any other highly gifted
writer.

Here are two samples of the straight narrative with
their flaws:

> In reality, of course, he was searching, searching
> with a hunger that had already something of desper-
> ation in it. (Dull purple prose.)

> About five weeks later Mary had a headache and
> took breakfast in bed. (A brief event set in an over-
> long, vague time period.)

It seems impossible to imagine C. S. Lewis writing
those two flimsy sentences in one five-page short story.
It is doubtful that one could find two such mediocre
sentences in all the rest of Lewis's fiction put together.
He didn't write inept prose.

In the last sentence of the story, a man's body fell
down into a quarry full of thick fog, and it made a tem-
porary rift in the fog before it hit the bottom. It is most
unlikely that Lewis would have imagined that a falling
body makes a rift in fog. He had a keen eye for nature.
Lewis would have seen this bit of description as a fiction-
writer's gaffe, and he would have chuckled over it.

As if that weren't enough, near the end of the story
Lewis purportedly wrote this sentence:

> "Do you see that?" shouted the violent stranger.

I can't help responding: "Did he write that?"

Now that we have "The Man Born Blind" in print, an old anecdote takes on new interest. In 1965, Walter Hooper, Owen Barfield, and seven others contributed to publisher Jock Gibb's collection of essays called *Light on C. S. Lewis*. Hooper began his part by telling that C. S. Lewis threw most of his own books and articles in the trash and forgot about them. When Hooper became his secretary, he said, he showed Lewis a list of his publications.

"Did *I* write all these?" Lewis asked, and then accused Hooper of inventing most of them.[10] They loved to josh each other.

So it is that the first person to accuse Walter Hooper of inflating the Lewis corpus was C. S. Lewis himself, according to Walter Hooper. Of course, that anecdote itself could be apocryphal. Whether that possibility spoils the irony or only increases the irony is a matter of opinion. But apocryphal anecdotes are of minor significance compared to apocryphal writings.

Walter Hooper's book *Past Watchful Dragons* (New York: Macmillan, 1979) features about twenty-six pages of Lewis's writing about Narnia not included in Lewis's own books. Hooper owns the handwritten documents. Professor Joe R. Christopher pointed out to me that the passage Hooper identifies as the very genesis of Narnia (printed on pages 29-30 of *Past Watchful Dragons* and page 238 of *C. S. Lewis: A Biography*) was found by Hooper on the back of *The Dark Tower* manuscript he rescued from the bonfire. Hooper states this clearly on page 238. This ties the authenticity of Hooper's dull but financially valuable Narnia documents to the authenticity of *The Dark Tower* and brings them into serious question. It also casts a shadow upon Hooper's otherwise unsupported claim that Lewis first started his Narnian stories in 1939 (rather than 1948). As a result, it increases my doubt about the dependability of Hooper's sections in the biography and all the rest of Hooper's products.

Once readers start to suspect that there are insertions, deletions, and revisions in some of Lewis's published works today, any odd passage is apt to look suspect if its history does not demonstrate that it is pure Lewis. For example, fifty of Lewis's letters to Arthur Greeves were not kept with the main group and were channeled to the public later through Walter Hooper, who got them from the wife of a cousin of Arthur Greeves.

In the letter dated 30 October 1955, C. S. Lewis wrote to his old bachelor friend Arthur Greeves about his future 1956 marriage to Joy Davidman. "The 'reality' would be, from my point of view, adultery and therefore mustn't happen. (An easy resolution when one doesn't in the least want it.)"

This letter may be genuine, but it contradicts what friends on the scene thought they were observing at the time. They thought they saw Lewis in love. ("I smell marriage in the air.")[11]

Was the Lewis marriage real? The marriage is still an embarrassment to some people, and the twenty-year fuss about it is an embarrassment to others. Now it has recently become a popular source of romantic inspiration for the general public. What is the truth about C. S. Lewis's love life? That is the subject of chapter 6, "Will the Real Mrs. Lewis Stand Up."

Chapter 5, Notes
1. *Time*, 8 September 1947.
2. Sometime before this Walter Hooper published his own attempt at a new Screwtape letter, "Hell and Immorality," in *Breakthrough*, 6-8 (no date). According to Joan Ostling in *C. S. Lewis: An Annotated Checklist*, this letter attacks the cult of the anti-hero but lacks Lewis's wit.
3. On page 191 of *C. S. Lewis: A Biography* (1974), Walter Hooper claimed that C. S. Lewis got his idea for Screwtape after the 8 a.m. communion

he attended on 15 July 1940. That date was a Monday, not a Sunday. Lewis attended communion on Sundays.

4. The following words from "Screwtape Turning Forty" in the Autumn 1980 issue of *Mythlore* had no effect and the important Lewis letter remained unpublished:

"The *Screwtape Letters* letter is one of the most interesting that we have from Lewis's hand. In addition to giving samples of what the devil might say to readers in his future book, Lewis gives a vivid sense, in his chatty way, of the tensions of World War II England. He combines this with his perpetual attention to human nature and literature and history. This is the interrupted two-day letter in which he observed (just before Screwtape was hatched) that he would be useless as a schoolteacher or policeman because of his tendency to become almost convinced by patent falsehoods presented unflinchingly.

"Lewis claimed here that he was especially slow at grading essay examinations because if a student with bold, mature handwriting claimed that Wordsworth wrote *Paradise Lost* he would feel a need to check to make sure that the student was wrong. Throughout this letter *deception* (both innocent and diabolical) versus truth is the apparently accidental theme. The sooner this July 20-21 letter is printed in its entirety, the better for Lewis readers."

5. C. S. Lewis, *The Screwtape Letters* (West Chicago: Lord and King Associates, 1976), 22.

6. Ibid., 42.

7. C. S. Lewis, *Letters to an American Lady* (Grand Rapids, Mich.: Wm. B. Eerdmans Publishing Co., 1967), 120-22.

8. Lewis's words at the end of Letter XII, on page 61 of the original Macmillan edition: "Indeed the safest road to Hell is the gradual one—the gentle slope, soft underfoot."

9. C. S. Lewis, *The Dark Tower and Other Stories*, ed. Walter Hooper (New York: Harcourt Brace Jovanovich, 1977), 11.

10. Walter Hooper, "A Bibliography of the Writings of C. S. Lewis" in *Light on C. S. Lewis*, ed. Jocelyn Gibb (New York: Harcourt, Brace & World, 1965), 117. Gibb was Managing Director of the Geoffrey Bles publishing firm.

11. Chad Walsh, "Afterword," in C. S. Lewis, *A Grief Observed* (New York: Bantam Books, 1976), 140.

WILL THE REAL MRS. LEWIS STAND UP

W hen he was six-teen years old, C. S. Lewis bragged to his friend Arthur Greeves about "the great event." A pretty girl from Belgium had agreed to make love with him.[1]

When he was thirty-two years old and reviewing the adolescent letters, he confessed that the big conquest had been make-believe, not reality. He hoped that his repentance could be complete without anyone except himself and Greeves ever knowing about it, because he would be mortified otherwise. Perhaps he didn't realize how common such lying is among boys.[2]

Ironically, seventy years after the non-event with the Belgian girl, C. S. Lewis might be mortified to know that some people are offended by the idea that he had "the great event" with his wife; some people are offended by the idea that he didn't have "the great event" with his wife; and some people are offended that it is an issue.

But perhaps C. S. Lewis would not be mortified now; perhaps he would smile ruefully at the joke fate played on him. Throughout his entire life and ever since, his private love-life has been one long story of tall tales, white·lies, discretion, denials, temptation, mistakes, and apparent timidity. Yet he has emerged as a romantic figure in spite of himself.

It is clear that when C. S. Lewis was only nineteen, recovering from the wounds of World War I, he became intensely involved with Mrs. Janie Moore, a handsome woman old enough to be his mother. Before long they began living together. His brother Warren used the word *infatuation*, and their father used the word *affair*. C. S. Lewis said little about the arrangement and kept it secret from university friends for a long time. Mrs. Moore was an aggressive, selfish, highly opinionated woman with few interests and a hysterical temperament, but she was outgoing and hospitable. Her nickname for her ex-husband, who was still living, was "The Beast." Her own nickname was Minto, the name of a kind of candy she particularly enjoyed.

C. S. Lewis's father felt that his son was an impetuous, kindhearted creature who let himself get caught by a needy woman who had "been through the mill." Worse yet, so long as Albert Lewis supported C. S. Lewis through his extended university studies, he was also unwillingly giving to Mrs. Moore and her daughter. The widowed father longed for his son's affection and loyalty, and he bitterly resented the obvious fact that Minto came first. She was possessive and domineering.

Whatever infatuation there ever was between C. S. Lewis and Minto Moore, it had certainly cooled on his side by the time he became a Christian, and probably long before. But, like many people caught in an unsatisfactory marriage, C. S. Lewis did not abandon his acquired family. He stayed with Minto Moore until she died of old age in 1951. So in a negative sense she was the first Mrs. C. S. Lewis, in cost and burden to C. S. Lewis, if not in meaning and name. She was one of the most uncongenial and inappropriate living partners he could have found.[3]

A wonderfully appropriate woman was drawn into C. S. Lewis's life in 1941. Her name was Ruth Pitter, and she was an attractive Londoner who supported herself by gathering wildflowers and painting their likeness on black tea trays. The daughter of inner-city educators, she was an artist with words as well as with paints; and she often worked out poems in her mind while she painted her delicate flower designs. She had an extremely keen eye and ear. She made a success of her wildflower painting until war shortages closed down her business, and she eventually became the first woman to win the Queen's Medal for Poetry. She published several books of poetry and won many honors.[4] But she did not win at love.

Ruth Pitter, along with hundreds of thousands of others, listened to C. S. Lewis's radio talks about Christianity during the Second World War. She listened simply because he was so entertaining; but before she knew it she was hooked and became a Christian. Eventually she found someone who could arrange for her to meet Lewis at the university. After he sampled her poetry for the first time, he said, "Why didn't someone tell me?" Although he had been working at poetry ever since he was a small child, she was a better poet than he was; and they both knew it.[5] He eagerly consulted her about his poems, and she gave him advice. His letters to her fill an album an inch thick in the Bodleian Library. She could have asked a great price for them, but she treasured them so much that she couldn't sell them. She donated them instead.

Ruth Pitter was so smitten by C. S. Lewis that she left London and bought a house in Long Crendon, about twelve miles from Oxford, in hopes of becoming Mrs. Lewis.[6] There she tactfully waited for him to respond to her presence, but he never came to visit her as often as she would have liked. He and Warren and friends of theirs enjoyed her greatly, but Lewis never courted her. The closest he came to it was to say to his friend Hugo Dyson, "I am not a man for marriage, but if I were I would ask Ruth Pitter." Alone and blind in her old age, Ruth Pitter still smiled about that.

Then an event that Lewis called "tragi-comical" occurred.[7] A hotel keeper's wife from Ramsgate called him and asked when he was going to pay Mrs. Hooker's bill, which was overdue. Who was this Mrs. Hooker, he asked, and why should he be paying her bills?

"But she's your *wife*!"

It turned out that at about the time of Minto Moore's death, early in 1951, a woman named Mrs. Hooker had started running up bills and borrowing money on the strength of her claim that she was marrying C. S. Lewis. It had worked quite a while before someone finally contacted Lewis to collect.

The hotel keeper's wife called the police as soon as she finished talking to C. S. Lewis, and in early May he had to appear to testify against his supposed wife in Ramsgate police court. He had never been to a law court before, and it appalled him to see a fellow creature at bay, with no way of escape. If this is what a just trial is like, he exclaimed, what in the name of all devils must an unjust trial be like?

It was not that Lewis saw any innocence in his purported wife. She was a confidence artist with twenty-one previous convictions. She's a bad woman, he observed. But he pitied her.

Lewis met some of the witnesses who had lost money to Mrs. Hooker, and their spirit impressed him. Not one of them said anything vindictive like "I hope she gets it in the neck." They all expressed sorrow, instead, that an educated woman like Mrs. Hooker chose to ruin her life with lies and thievery.

"Here, surely," Lewis reflected, "is an occasion of joy." He had to go to court twice, and it has been said that he also visited Mrs. Hooker in Holloway prison. Whether his compassion helped her any or not, it obviously did him good.

Roger Lancelyn Green has told the story of another would-be Mrs. Lewis from that same period of time.[8] She wrote often to Lewis, trying to attract his attention with gaudily decorated envelopes. Like Mrs. Hooker, she told people that she and C. S. Lewis were engaged to be married. She didn't defraud people, but she did finally put an announcement of their wedding in the papers and came to the Kilns to collect her husband. Fortunately for Lewis he was not home, and she was taken away and disappeared from his life.

In this same general period Helen Joy Davidman Gresham arrived from the United States to consult C. S. Lewis about her writing and her dreadful marriage problems. She invited him to meet her at lunch at the Eastgate Hotel, and they enjoyed each other from the start. After six months in England, Joy went home in January of 1953, agreed to a divorce as Lewis had advised, and returned to England in November with her two sons.

On 24 January 1954, C. S. Lewis invited Ruth Pitter and Joy Davidman to lunch with him at the Eastgate Hotel, so they could meet and become friends. In discussing that luncheon party years later, Ruth Pitter has said, "It was not pleasant. It was not. I can tell you that much."[9] She wrote out a description and put it in a safe place, not to be opened for fifty years.

Like Ruth Pitter, Joy Davidman was a stimulating and witty intellectual who had been led to Christianity by Lewis's writing. But like Minto Moore, Joy Davidman was a needy divorced mother and an aggressive and abrasive woman. It was a powerful combination. Gradually Joy Davidman managed to make herself an important part of C. S. Lewis's life, although few of his friends liked her.[10]

It was not until Joy Davidman was denied further residence in England early in 1956 that C. S. Lewis decided to marry her in a civil ceremony. It took place on 23 April 1956, and was kept secret.[11] It made Joy and her two sons legal residents of England permanently. That is all that Lewis intended at the time.

A month or two after that secret wedding, Joy began to have leg pain. Doctors said it was rheumatism. Six months after the secret wedding, the leg snapped because it was eaten through by cancer; and the cancer had spread. In November Lewis wrote to a correspondent in the United States, "I may be soon, in rapid succession, a bridegroom and a widower."[12]

In December he decided to make the April wedding into more than he had intended. Without giving any clarification, he announced in the Times on Christmas Eve, "A marriage has taken place between Professor C. S. Lewis of Magdalene College, Cambridge, and Mrs. Joy Gresham, now a patient in Churchill Hospital, Oxford." Readers assumed, of course, that it was a December wedding.

At last there was an official Mrs. C. S. Lewis. She was forty and he was fifty-seven. Both of them had stated in their writing that divorced Christians may not remarry when a previous spouse is still living, and Joy's first husband, Bill Gresham, was still very much alive although Joy herself was almost dead.

C. S. Lewis thought about the fact that William Gresham had been married twice before he married Joy and that they had not been Christians when they married. He thought this seemed to invalidate Joy's first marriage in the eyes of the church, thus making it possible for him to marry her in a church ceremony. But the Bishop of Oxford told him that such remarriage was not allowed by the church at that time. [13]

C. S. Lewis heard that an ex-student of his who had become an Anglican priest, Peter Bide, was sometimes granted miraculous answers to his prayers for healing. The doctors gave Joy no hope at all, and the best that could be wished for was reduced suffering before death. So Lewis asked Peter Bide to come to Oxford to lay hands on Joy and pray for her healing. When Bide came, Lewis brought up the subject of Christian marriage. Bide thought that Lewis's reasoning about the matter was sound, and he believed that Joy's ardent desire to have her marriage solemnized by the church should be honored. He did not have the right to perform the ceremony without the permission of the Bishop of Oxford, but he did so anyway. On 21 March 1957, the Christian marriage ceremony took place at Joy's hospital bedside.

The amazing healing that took place in the months after that is a much-told story. Warren Lewis wrote that it was obvious they not only loved, but were in love with each other. C. S. Lewis declared that he had in his sixties the joy that most men have in their twenties. Joy wrote to friends that he was a great lover. They took a belated honeymoon to Ireland. Lewis later referred to Joy as his daughter and mother, pupil and teacher, subject and sovereign, comrade, friend, shipmate, fellow-soldier, and mistress. She referred to herself triumphantly as Mrs. C. S. Lewis.

There is no question about the fact that Lewis's marriage was a great disappointment to his old friend J. R. R. Tolkien, a staunch Roman Catholic who disliked Joy in the first place and could not approve of marriage to a divorced American in any case. Lewis had compounded the damage by not informing Tolkien of the marriage, letting him find out as the news spread. Tolkien's resentment of Joy Lewis faintly echoed Albert Lewis's resentment of Minto Moore; he felt that C. S. Lewis let himself get taken in by the wrong people.

In *Through Joy and Beyond: A Pictorial Biography of C. S. Lewis*, Hooper defends C. S. Lewis by insisting, "For religious as well as physical reasons, Lewis's marriage was not consummated."[14] He explains that Lewis's description of the marriage in his 1961 account of his eventual bereavement, *A Grief Observed*, was partly fiction. The reason Lewis identified his wife only by her first initial in this book, and originally used the pen name N. W. Clerk, was simply that it was not a true account, according to Hooper. In contrast, Warren Lewis claimed that it described his brother's marriage exactly. It was Lewis's most personal book.

On 20 December 1961, C. S. Lewis wrote to his ex-student and old friend Dom Bede Griffiths, a Roman Catholic priest in India, that something interesting had happened. When Joy died, Lewis had prayed that God would take away the lifelong burden of his sexual nature. Then he became free of all sexual desire. And now he could recall fully and gratefully the act of love in his marriage without any more desire or arousal. It is doubtful Lewis would write such a confidence to a priest about a marriage that was never consummated.

Because *C. S. Lewis: A Biography* had two authors, it has two opposing views of the marriage. Roger Lancelyn Green wrote a convincing chapter attesting to its vitality and completeness.[15] But Walter Hooper claimed that in 1930 C. S. Lewis identified himself as one who cannot ever marry.[16] Hooper does not give source or explanation. He does go on to reason that it was the 1917 promise to Paddy Moore that outwardly enforced bachelorhood upon Lewis. However, Hooper assures readers, Lewis preferred living with Mrs. Moore to marriage. Moreover, Hooper claims that in 1963 Lewis confided to him that he had always been a bachelor at heart. (Not, perhaps, the most gallant remark for a widower to make.)

Relatively few people were much interested in the pros and cons of C. S. Lewis's brief marriage for the first twenty years after his death, even after the 1974 biography and Chad Walsh's 1976 essay about the marriage at the back of the Bantam edition of *A Grief Observed*. But a film changed all that.

Joy Davidman had won a chance at Hollywood scriptwriting in 1939 and spent a few months in California writing for M-G-M. Her scripts were not accepted, so she gave up and returned to New York. Little could she have guessed that forty-five years later someone else would write a successful filmscript about her and that hundreds of thousands of people would see it and feel great admiration and anguish for her. The film won "best single television drama" and "best television actress" awards from the British Academy of Film and Television. It appeared on American television in 1986. It is called *Shadowlands*.

Shadowlands is a drama based upon the marriage of C. S. Lewis and Joy Davidman. In order to squeeze it all into ninety minutes and keep costs down, several years of events had to be condensed into three years in the film. Lewis, excellently acted by Joss Ackland, neither looks nor acts much like the real man; he has become soft, blue-eyed, and grandfatherly. His Christian faith is only tentative at the end of the film after Joy has died. All he really has left is Joy's two adorable little boys with whom he has to face the future. In fact, of course, C. S. Lewis's faith was far more vigorous than that; and his stepsons were in their late teens. In the film Lewis sat out in the snow alone when Joy died; in real life she died in July. The film is not a serious documentary.

The film succeeds, however, in making people fall in love with the love between C. S. Lewis and Joy Davidman. Their story is beautified, of course. The Kilns becomes a house set on a hill, the interior becomes charming, and those who live there are no longer chain smokers. Everything in the story suggests quality. Everything makes us wish we were there. Especially Joy.

In *Shadowlands* Joy Davidman is transformed from a brassy New Yorker with hornrimmed glasses and rather dowdy looks into a luminously beautiful, truly exquisite woman of good-natured refinement and radiant sensitivity. She is irresistible. And this is the image that most of the public will have of Mrs. C. S. Lewis for years to come. Distortion of the facts about the Lewises is used to communicate quickly and simply the truth of their love and the tragedy of their parting. C. S. Lewis has been given the lovely actress Claire Bloom to be his lawful wedded wife in the public mind, for better or worse. He would no doubt be amazed.

Long before the film was planned, Claire Bloom took part in another C. S. Lewis project. She read Lewis's book *Prince Caspian* for Caedmon Records in 1979, and her photo and career credits appear on the back of the album along with an essay by Walter Hooper.

There by the face now known to the public as that of Mrs. C. S. Lewis, Walter Hooper states, "I was Lewis's secretary at the end of his life, and after his death in 1963 I inherited his papers." How could the American Walter Hooper, who had only met C. S. Lewis on a visit to England in 1963, have inherited his papers then? That is the subject of chapter 7, "Forging a Friendship."

Chapter 6, Notes
1. C. S. Lewis, *They Stand Together* (New York: Macmillan, 1979), 65.
2. Ibid., 424.
3. On 17 January 1951, Warren Lewis reflected in his diary about how Mrs. Moore had kept C. S. Lewis from both bachelorhood and marriage. His bitter comments are located on pages 236-69 of *Brothers and Friends* (San Francisco: Harper & Row, 1982). There are related comments on pages 224 and 265.
4. Ruth Pitter was installed as a Companion of Literature along with Arthur Koestler and Lord Clarke in 1974.
5. Ruth Pitter has consented to the reprinting of her poem "Swifts" here, from her 1975 collection *End of Drought*, published by Barrie & Jenkins of London, now superseded by Hutchinson & Co. Ltd.

Low over the warm roof of an old barn,
Down in a flash to the water, up and away with a cry
And a wild swoop and a sharp turn
And a fever of life under a thundery sky,
So they go over, so they go by.

And high and high and high in the diamond light,
Soaring and crying in sunshine when heaven is bare,
With the pride of life in their strong flight
And a rapture of love to lift them and carry them there,
High and high in the diamond air.

And away with the summer, away like the spirit of glee,
Flashing and calling, strong on the wing, and wild in their play,

With a high cry to the high sea,
And a heart for the south, a heart for the diamond day,
So they go over, so go away.

6. Personal conversation with Ruth Pitter on 19 June 1984, in her home at 71 Chilton Road, Long Crendon.

7. Lewis's account in an unpublished letter to Dom Bede Griffiths, 17 May 1952.

8. Roger Lancelyn Green and Walter Hooper, C. S. Lewis: A Biography (London: Collins, 1974), 258-59.

9. Stephen Schofield, In Search of C. S. Lewis (South Plainfield, N. J.: Bridge, 1983), 114.

10. The story of Joy Davidman's life is told by Lyle Dorsett in And God Came In (New York: Macmillan, 1983).

11. C. S. Lewis's first letter to me was written on 24 April 1956, the day after his civil marriage to Joy Davidman. He did not mention her existence then or when we met on July 20. During our conversation on July 20 he laughed at the warning I had received from Dr. Clyde Kilby that he avoided women. He told me how disappointed he was that his novel Till We Have Faces was meeting a cool reception; but he did not mention the identity of Joy Davidman, to whom he had dedicated that book.

12. C. S. Lewis, Letters to an American Lady (Grand Rapids, Mich.: Wm. B. Eerdmans Publishing Co., 1967), 61.

13. On page 536 of They Stand Together, Walter Hooper claims that "Lewis himself was wary of such casuistry" and that other people have tried to reason away Joy's marriage to William Lindsay Gresham in order to validate her marriage to C. S. Lewis. In fact, C. S. Lewis reasoned away Joy's marriage to Gresham in his 25 June 1957 letter to Dorothy Sayers, in which he celebrated his joyful marriage. This letter appears on pages 143-45 of Walter Hooper's book, Through Joy and Beyond (New York: Macmillan, 1982).

14. Hooper, Through Joy and Beyond, 151.

15. Green and Hooper, C. S. Lewis, 257-78.

16. Ibid., 107.

FORGING A FRIENDSHIP

"Like Father, Like Son" is the perfect title for H. W. Kelley's happy two-page article about C. S. Lewis and Walter Hooper that appeared in the Christmas issue of *The Anglican Digest* in 1982. Lewis once remarked in print that perhaps there is nothing more astonishing than the discovery that there are people very, very like oneself. Walter Hooper is so much like his mentor C. S. Lewis, Kelley exclaims, that as you sit in his living room chatting with him you keep forgetting that he is not Lewis.

Hooper used to live with C. S. Lewis, Kelley continues. Most books by or about C. S. Lewis since his death have been edited, written, or annotated by Hooper. The writings of the two merge seamlessly, Kelley thinks. Hooper resembles the bronze bust of C. S. Lewis on a pedestal in his living room. His voice sounds like Lewis's recorded voice.

Hooper starts most days by dipping a nib pen into an inkwell, Kelley adds, as Lewis did it. Lewis's furnishings must have been similar to Hooper's. Hooper's books resemble Lewis's books. Lewis would have liked Hooper's flowers. A day spent visiting Hooper has the texture of a day straight out of a Lewis biography, Kelley continues.

Lewis even referred to Hooper as "the son I should have had," and when Lewis died on 22 November 1963, Hooper found that he had been designated Lewis's literary executor. Kelley was obviously enchanted with Walter Hooper.[1] Many people are.

One thing Kelley missed was that Hooper even smokes cigarettes in the special way that C. S. Lewis did. In the printed text of a speech Hooper gave in California once, he said, "Lewis didn't use an ash tray, but took his cigarette and flicked it like this. Did you see that? I've been doing it all day."[2]

A member of his audience later wrote a report published in the bulletin *Mythprint*, "the gentle, almost murmuring voice of Father Walter Hooper, relating another anecdote of our Chosen Rabbi C. S. Lewis, perhaps accompanied by that marvelous S-shaped gesture guaranteed to seed the carpet with ashes from the August Cigarettes of Professor Lewis (or his own). . . ."[3]

When one recalls that Walter Hooper's 1979 seminars across the United States were called "A Visit with C. S. Lewis," it seems fitting.

Once Hooper had become the famous son of his home town, the *Reidsville Review* in North Carolina printed his reflections about some of his formative experiences.[4] One was his teaching post with the English department at the University of Kentucky, where he says he taught the 1960-1962 terms. During his first month in Lexington he served as night watchman in the Henry Clay house, sleeping in Henry Clay's own bed. When he found better lodging, he says, he was spared the embarrassment of waking up to find a child pointing at him and asking if he were Henry Clay—or Henry Clay's ghost.

From Henry Clay to C. S. Lewis.

Hooper says he took over C. S. Lewis's own bedroom in 1963 when Lewis was too ill to go upstairs. Lewis informed Hooper that Hooper was now sleeping under the very blanket that nine-year-old C. S. Lewis had slept under at boarding school in 1908 after his mother died. Hooper says he treasures that blanket from C. S. Lewis's childhood to this day.[5]

"I begin with an apology," Hooper said in a formal address about Lewis in 1975. Although in print he calls himself the world's foremost authority on Lewis, in person he is remarkably humble. (Hooper has been thought of by some as a man of overweening modesty.)

"I am reminded of the funeral arranged for Abraham Lincoln in Springfield, Illinois," he continued. "Because the great man could not himself be there to speak, and because a great many of his friends had died as well, his old dog Fido was brought, so to speak, out of mothballs. *He* was alive. Now I think you must receive me as something of a 'Fido.'. . . For that is all I claim to be."[6]

Victor Searcher's three-hundred-page volume *The Farewell to Lincoln*, which includes every verified detail of the funeral services in the capital, the twelve-day journey to Springfield, and the burial there, makes no mention of an old dog named Fido attending the funeral. The closest one can find is Lincoln's old horse Robin following the hearse in Springfield.

That's all right. It seems that Hooper wasn't teaching English at the University of Kentucky and sleeping in Henry Clay's bed in 1960 anyway. He was teaching high school in North Carolina.[7] But Hooper really did teach in Kentucky later. In fact, he still taught there in the spring and fall semesters of 1963. That is the year when, according to his entries in reference books, he was serving as C. S. Lewis's private secretary in Oxford.

In the spring of 1963, Hooper sat in on lectures by Dr. Robert O. Evans about contemporary British novels. Dr. Evans has edited collections of essays about both Graham Greene and William Golding. Hooper talked with Dr. Evans about the possibility of writing a doctoral dissertation on Lewis when he passed qualifying examinations for the doctoral program.

In the summer of 1963 Evans was in Oxford teaching Shakespeare to a group of student tourists when Hooper was attending a different summer course for visiting students there.[8] The two saw each other a few times before Dr. Evans left Oxford in early August, unable to meet Lewis for himself because of Lewis's severe illness. He had enjoyed Hooper's enthusiasm about the great man, which came to happy fruition; and he wrote to both the *Los Angeles Times* and the Director of the Southern California C. S. Lewis Society sixteen years later[9] to vouch for Hooper when the *Times* raised some questions about Hooper's career after his public presentation in the Pasadena Civic Auditorium.[10]

It was the well-intentioned 1979 letter from Dr. Evans that revealed the fact that Walter Hooper was living at a summer school program in Oxford in the summer of 1963. If Evans's memory is correct, Hooper was at Exeter College attending a busy course that lasted from July 1 to August 9, including lectures, tutorials, and excursions. All of Hooper's accounts of his activities that fateful summer leave out the key fact that he was a student then. Summer school changes the whole story.

One of Hooper's fond anecdotes about C. S. Lewis took place when Lewis and Hooper attended church together "one Easter."[11] In 1963 Easter fell on April 14, and Hooper had not yet gone to England. Hooper spent the summer in England and returned to Kentucky for the fall semester. Lewis died in November. It appears impossible that Lewis and Hooper could ever have attended church together on Easter.

When this and other discrepancies in Walter Hooper's claims about his education, career, and relationship to C. S. Lewis were aired in the summer 1978 issue of *Christianity & Literature*, loyal friends came to his defense. Owen Barfield, the other Lewis Estate Trustee, complained about "waspish innuendo . . . offensive and probably libelous insinuations."[12] (Indeed, his legal firm later sent me a letter threatening to sue.)[13] Eugene McGovern, editor of *CSL: Bulletin of the New York C. S. Lewis Society* joined Barfield with a letter that declared, "Preposterous scenario . . . none of Lindskoog's business." James Como, editor of *C. S. Lewis at the Breakfast Table* sent in a letter for publication (the editor decided against it) that snorted, "Back-fence gossip."

A bit later bookdealer Nigel Sustins of Surrey stated the case for Hooper more calmly in the *Canadian C. S. Lewis Journal*:

> Walter Hooper does not need to verify his "credentials." The length of time spent with Lewis before his death is immaterial. It is for work done since Lewis's death that we owe Walter Hooper such an immense debt; for painstaking scholarship,[14] and for years spent helping countless individuals all over the world wishing to know more of Lewis.[15]

Unimportant as historical details are, from that point of view, it is harmless enough to note that according to his friends C. S. Lewis did not flick ashes with an elegant S-curve; and Lewis certainly did not look or sound much like Hooper. More important, Lewis did not refer to Hooper as "the son I should have had."

The story about that remark is located on page 303 in C. S. Lewis: A Biography where Hooper claims that Lewis said it to his housekeeper Mrs. Miller. Apparently Lewis's remark about the son he should have had was just a remark he should have made. After the biography came out, Mr. and Mrs. Miller vehemently denied that Lewis ever said anything like it. In fact, they said that C. S. Lewis was hoping that Hooper would not return in 1964. Hooper had been eager and attentive, but Lewis felt one dose was enough.[16]

Although many claims about the affinity between C. S. Lewis and Walter Hooper do not hold up, one of the most important of them is emphatically true. Hooper writes with a pen like Lewis's, and his writing looks like Lewis's. (Although Hooper types, he says he writes so much by hand that he uses two quarts of ink a year.)

Among Walter Hooper's talents is marvelously neat, controlled penmanship. His writing can appear identical to that of C. S. Lewis. In his film Through Joy and Beyond it seems to be Hooper's own hand that viewers see writing out words of young Lewis in appropriate script for that age. Apparently Hooper can reproduce Lewis's hand-writing at various stages of life. It is doubtful that anyone except handwriting experts could distinguish between Lewis's handwriting and Walter Hooper's that looks like it.

Many people must have remarked about the uncanny resemblance. In response to one correspondent, Hooper made an amazing claim. Someone once accused Hooper of intentionally imitating Lewis's penmanship, he said; but, in fact, it was C. S. Lewis himself who first noticed the similarity. Lewis would dictate letters to Hooper and sign them. But eventually he had Hooper sign the letters for him because the handwriting looked the same.[17]

In all the decades when Warren Lewis was his brother's secretary, he was not given the responsibility of signing letters with his brother's signature. Such abandon with a brand new friend is puzzling. If any questionable 1963 C. S. Lewis letters should ever turn up and be checked for their authenticity, their being written and signed by Hooper instead of Lewis would simply illustrate his claim that Lewis had instructed him to do the signing. It is a troublesome situation.

Furthermore, for the literary executor of an important estate to own a private cache of papers from the great writer and also to be able to imitate that writer's penmanship is a potentially dangerous opportunity for fraud. Fortunately, Hooper has been open and frank about his ability to duplicate Lewis's handwriting. Surely some people in Hooper's position might have been tempted to keep such a capacity a secret and to supplement their collection of genuine Lewis documents with new ones of their own creation.

Two letters that Walter Hooper penned for C. S. Lewis in 1963 are available for examination. They are both located in the Marion E. Wade Center, and they were both published in Lewis's *Letters to an American Lady.* The first one was dated July 27 and began, "Jack asked me to tell you that letter writing is physically impossible, his fingers jerk and twitch so. His physical crisis has greatly disordered his intelligence and he is vividly aware of living in a world of hallucinations." Hooper accidentally switched at that point to Lewis's exact words to the lady, and signed the letter Jack and posted it that way.

On August 10 Hooper wrote to the American lady again for Lewis, beginning, "I am Professor C. S. Lewis's secretary writing to tell you some facts concerning Professor Lewis's present state of health. I felt you were entitled to this history. I trust that you will not mind it coming from my hand, but so it must." He signed it Walter Hooper.[18]

The lady, Mrs. Mary Shelburne, received one more letter from C. S. Lewis before he died, dated August 30. It was in his own handwriting, and he told her that because his brother Warren was away, he had no help with correspondence and could not write much. (That is strange in light of the fact that Walter Hooper says he was Lewis's companion-secretary until late September.)

The peculiar thing about Walter Hooper's two letters to the American lady is not that they look as if they were written by C. S. Lewis, but that they definitely do not look as if they were written by Lewis. At that point Walter Hooper's script was larger and more open than that of C. S. Lewis, very much the standard American handwriting taught in United States' schools. Such script is the ideal for American teachers, and indeed Hooper's B.A. and M.A. were both in education; he tried his hand as a sixth-grade teacher at an elementary school in Chapel Hill, North Carolina, in 1956-1957, and then taught in a boys' boarding school in Arden for two years in 1959-1961. His penmanship was just right.

The 1963 handwriting in letters to Mrs. Shelburne was not a fluke. In 1965 Hooper's handwriting was still much the same as in 1963. But it changed gradually, and by 1975 it looked like the handwriting of C. S. Lewis.

The fact that Hooper's penmanship is like Lewis's is far more important than when it became that way. And the fact that Hooper is an Anglican priest is far more important than where and when he obtained his training.[19] His accounts have varied, but it is true that he is a priest.[20] Whether or not he was ever in any sense C. S. Lewis's personal literary assistant who helped him with his writing is another matter. That is a more recent claim.[21] And the extent of his friendship with Lewis has always been unclear.

Another friend of C. S. Lewis from the American South, Sheldon Vanauken (author of A *Severe Mercy*), answered a set of questions about his friendship with C. S. Lewis in a 1979 interview that was never published. Pages 2 through 4 survive, and Vanauken allows them to be included here for the light they shed on some of Lewis's personal relationships.[22]

Interview with Sheldon Vanauken

Q: That's very interesting. You did know Mr. Lewis rather well then, didn't you?

A: Not as well of course as some of the Inklings and his old friends. But it's all in my book. On those visits to Cambridge I told you about, I felt we were very close indeed.

Q: Was there any special reason for that?

A. Yes. A combination of things. All the correspondence about my wife's death and about grief. And now Lewis being married and facing *his* wife's death. Bound to make us closer.

Q: You said in your book that he said he was in love with her when you met in Oxford that year. Did he say more about it at Cambridge?

A: I don't recall a specific statement, but it was sort of an understood thing behind all our talk. Everything I said was based on the idea that he felt about Joy as I felt about Davy; and everything *he* said implied that, too. I don't doubt it at all.

Q: In Carpenter's book, *The Inklings*, there is a slight suggestion that Lewis's marriage was never consummated. What is your opinion of that?

A: I don't believe it. Not for a minute! What Carpenter said was that there wasn't any evidence that it had been consummated. That's rather silly. How many marriages can you think of where there is evidence? In fact, what evidence can there be? Even children don't really *prove* anything, do they? Unless they have the Romanov nose or something. Even in the old days when the groom used to hang a blood-stained sheet out of the window, he could have pricked his finger or cut the throat of a mouse, couldn't he? Anyhow, look at those later letters in my book, when Joy was up and shooting pigeons. They sound like a consummated marriage to me. And, even more so, *A Grief Observed*.

Q: About that there's been a suggestion that *A Grief Observed* is fiction, as proved by his using a pseudonym.

A: Come on! That's nonsense! He has a frightful grief, so he writes of some other grief! Nonsense! He didn't publish any of his other fiction under a pseudonym. He wrote as N. W. Clerk because it was unbearably personal. Besides, the real proof is, he told me about it as his own grief in a letter I've lost; and I ordered it straight away from England, first printing. Anyway, no fiction was ever like that. Certainly not!

Q: Okay. Very convincing. Now, Mr. Vanauken, in *A Severe Mercy* you refer to some letters from Lewis that for one reason or another were not included, and you just now mentioned a lost letter. Can you tell me anything about the lost letters?

A: A little perhaps. There was a second letter on the question of homosexuality, as he had said he'd write after talking with others. I lent it to a homosexual student who wanted to copy it, and he lost it, unfortunately. As well as I remember, he came to the same conclusions. Then there was a letter, very agonized, about Joy's death. I decided it ought not to be saved and tore it up.

Q: How many letters would you say were lost or not retained by you?

A: Perhaps half a dozen or a bit more. All but that homosexual letter were late ones, after the "Severe Mercy" one. There was one I'd love to find again. It was about his heroine Orual in *Till We Have Faces* before it was published or even named perhaps. I used to put letters from him in his books, and I remember shifting this one into *Till We Have Faces* when I got it. I don't know what happened to it, unless I lent the book to someone and they stole it, blast them!

Q: The last letter in *A Severe Mercy* was dated June 1962. Was that the last letter from him?

A: Oh, no. Certainly not. There was at least one more in '62. I tried to space letters out so as not to burden him, you know. And there was one in early '63, the year of his death. By early I mean the first three or four months of the year. I had told him that I expected to be in England in the late summer and autumn, and he said he would be looking forward to seeing me. He talked a bit about how he was thinking of Joy, now that more time had gone.

Q: That was the very last one?

A: I think so, except for a note in November, the month he died, inviting me to tea at the Kilns.

Q: He was still able to write then?

A: Oh, yes. I didn't know of course that he'd been so ill in the summer, in hospital and all that. He may have said in the note that he'd been unwell, or perhaps that was when I was out there.

Q: He told you all about the illness that afternoon?

A: I don't know if it was "all" but it was a good deal. He told me he'd been out of his head and that they thought he was going to die. And some more about his present condition: why they couldn't operate. I could see he wasn't very well. He warned me he would doze off for a few seconds while we talked, and he did. It was frightening. I didn't think he was going to die in a matter of days—in fact, we arranged a second meeting in a fortnight—but I thought I would never come to England to see him again. But we got the tea together—we were alone in the house—and he was cheerful and even brisk at moments. But when that other meeting came due, he was dead.

Q: What did you and Lewis talk about?

A: Everything. It was actually a rather wonderful last meeting. It was blowing and raining outside and all snug within. We talked about Joy and Davy and meeting them again. He spoke of his recent article, "We Have No Right to Happiness." And about my booklet

"Encounter with Light," which he had seen long before. It was written in 1961, and he had let me use three of his letters to me in it, which is why they weren't copyrighted.[23]

Q: Anyone may use them?

A: That's right. I even excluded them from the copyright of A Severe Mercy, thinking Jack would have liked that. Anyway, he liked the booklet.

Q: Had Mr. Lewis ever mentioned Walter Hooper in his letters?

A: No. No reason why he should have done. When I had that last letter in '63, Walter Hooper hadn't come over yet, had he?

Q: But of course he told you that afternoon, when he was talking about the hospital, about Father Hooper's help and being his secretary afterwards?

A: No.

Q: Not at all? It says in the Biography that Lewis regarded him as the son he never had and all that. And Hooper was a fellow American, too.

A: Practically a neighbor: North Carolina, you know. But Jack didn't mention him.

Q: Why didn't he, do you think?

A: No idea. Jack may not have thought of Virginia and North Carolina being so close. Also, by then Walter had gone back to the States. Jack did talk about his brother, the Major, what a help he was with letters and all that.

Q: But no mention of Walter Hooper?

A: No.

Strange as it is that C. S. Lewis failed to mention his new companion-secretary to Sheldon Vanauken, it is even stranger that Lewis failed to mention him in his 1963 letters to old friends such as Arthur Greeves.

One assumes that Walter Hooper would not consciously exaggerate his closeness to C. S. Lewis, in light of the derision such behavior is apt to cause. (Wilfred Sheed's acerbic comment, "Claiming close friendship with the recent dead is a knavish trick" comes to mind.)[24] But the relationship most likely loomed larger in Hooper's thinking than in Lewis's. It was sometimes overstated in the early years. For example, on the dustjacket of *God in the Dock* (Lewis essays edited by Hooper), the American publisher stated "Walter Hooper, a long-time friend and for some years personal secretary of C. S. Lewis."

"Some years" was the term used on the British edition also. In early May of 1969 a friend of Warren Lewis wrote to the London *Times* on his behalf protesting that Walter Hooper had not been Lewis's secretary that long. The editor replied to her that Hooper was reducing his claim to one year, during which he lived at the Kilns with the Lewis brothers.

The idea that Hooper had lived at the Kilns with the Lewis brothers was not a new one. On the back of the book *Light on C. S. Lewis*[25] Hooper was identified thus: "An American scholar when he first met Lewis some ten years ago on a grant that enabled him to study Lewis's work, Hooper eventually became Lewis's secretary, and lived with him and his brother."[26]

Warren, who had never even met Walter Hooper until Hooper returned to England after Lewis's death, was exasperated. In Hooper's desire to appear to be one of Lewis's oldest and most intimate friends, Warren decided, he was guilty of a couple of "terminological inexactitudes."[27] He wrote to Hooper in protest.

From that time on, the two men seemed to be on a quiet collision course. What would eventually come of it? That is the subject of the next chapter, "They Fall Together."

Chapter 7, Notes

1. H. W. Kelley, "Like Father, Like Son," *The Anglican Digest*, December 1982, 8-9.
2. Walter Hooper, "Reminiscences," *Mythlore*, June 1976, 6-7. This is the text of the speech given 16 August 1975 but it has been heavily edited by Hooper, with the bonfire cut out.
3. Judith Brown, notes in *Mythprint: The Monthly Bulletin of the Mythopoeic Society*, November 1975, 9.
4. Barbara Terry, "From Reidsville to Oxford, England: A Fan Letter to Lewis Started It All," *Reidsville Review*, 26 May 1975.
5. Walter Hooper, "Introduction," in C. S. Lewis, *They Stand Together* (London: Collins, 1979), 9.
6. Hooper, "Reminiscences," 5.
7. "Upon leaving the Virginia Episcopal Seminary, Hooper was offered a teaching post at Christ School in Arden, N.C., a post which he held for two years." (Terry, "From Reidsville to Oxford.") Christ School was a boarding school for boys ages 13-18.
8. "A number of British Universities have combined since 1948 to organize annually a special programme of Summer Schools providing primarily for the needs of postgraduate students from the Universities of America, Europe and the British Commonwealth. About two-thirds of the students have come from the United States. . . . The Schools will last six weeks, and are recognized for Credits at American Universities and, subject to certain conditions, for grants under the GI Bill of Rights."

In 1963, the "British University Summer Schools" program was held at Stratford-upon-Avon, Edinburgh, and Oxford. The course at Oxford was made up of 120 students studying "History, Literature and the Arts of Seventeenth-Century England" at Exeter College from July 1 to August 9. The history and politics in the course included the early Stuarts and the Great Rebellion, the period from the Great Rebellion to the Revolution, and Seventeenth-century political ideas. The literature in this course included Donne and the metaphysical poets, Milton, and both Jacobean and Restoration drama.

It seems highly likely that this was the very course Hooper enjoyed in 1963. And it is possible that the "grant" he has referred to which allowed him to go to England was, in fact, the GI Bill of Rights, which funded

British Summer Schools for many young American men who had served
two years in the Army. A few scholarships were also available for the
course, and the deadline for scholarship applications was 1 March 1963.
The inclusive charge for room, board and tuition for the six-week course
was only 90 pounds (approximately $254).

9. Robert O. Evans, letter to William Geiger of Whittier College on 21
September 1979:

"To begin, I knew Walter Hooper when he was at UK. . . .

"In the summer of 1963 I was in residence at Lincoln College in Oxford,
lecturing on Shakespeare, in conjunction with the Stratford theatre, to
a group of foreign students, mostly Scandinavians. I knew Hooper was in
England, and my wife and I took the trouble to meet with him more than
once. He was at that time very enthusiastic about his meetings with Lewis,
though he was living in another Oxford college near Lincoln taking a
different summer course."

After his retirement a few years later, Dr. Evans expanded on those
memories: "I am virtually certain Hooper was living at the college then
and paying occasional visits to CSL at the house. Certainly he was not
CSL's private secretary in late July and early August when the program
was undertaken."

In a 4 April 1987 letter to me, Dr. Evans reminisced about Walter Hooper
and noted that he had "a rather chameleon quality," but that he never
seemed at all mendacious. "A Boswell-like quality," Dr. Evans observed,
"is strong in some students." Hooper, however, never gave Dr. Evans the
impression that he was planning to move in with C. S. Lewis nor that
he was going to become Lewis's secretary.

10. John Dart, "Questions Raised on C. S. Lewis Lore," *Los Angeles Times*,
24 March 1979, 30-31. This article balanced unanswered questions about
"the U.S.-born bachelor Anglican priest who is well established as a
gatekeeper for much of the Lewis lore and literature" with comments from
Walter Hooper and his supporters. Paul Ford, author of *Companion to
Narnia*, said that the questioning "detracts from the marvelous scholarship
that Walter has done, from Lewis himself. . . . There is a suspicion of
Walter that is unwarranted." Walter Hooper himself said, "I can't understand why anyone would want to poison the wells and sharpen the knives
and somehow separate those who admire Lewis."

11. James Como, "An Evening with Walter Hooper," *CSL: The Bulletin of the
New York C. S. Lewis Society*, July 1975, 6. Como introduced guest speaker
Walter Hooper at the 11 July 1975 meeting by reminding those present
of the Lewis books that Hooper had edited, his position as Executor of
the Estate, and the fact that Father Hooper is "the Society's best friend."

During his presentation Hooper told about hearing an Easter sermon with
C. S. Lewis and also said that Lewis saw women as more monogamous
than men. Hooper ventured that we seem to be already hearing cries of
frustration and outrage from women who have tried to flout this. In his
introduction to *The Dark Tower* (not yet published), Hooper revealed,
"Ransom anticipates the bitter and frenzied feminists of today."

Not a Genuinely Copied Signature After All? 113

This concern of Hooper's about ladies behaving themselves may be behind his 1974 characterization of Oxford philosopher Elizabeth Anscombe, who bested C. S. Lewis in informal debate about a point in *Miracles* in 1948. In *C. S. Lewis: A Biography* Hooper claims that Lewis told him privately that in fact Anscombe did not win her point after all, and Hooper attributes her apparent victory to unfair bullying. Given Lewis's reputation as a "butcher" even in friendly debate, his martyrdom at the hands of Anscombe is an odd proposal.

In James Como's 1979 collection *C. S. Lewis at the Breakfast Table*, Hooper told again about the debate and added "A few years later [a few years after 1948] when I met Miss Anscombe in the common room of Sommerville College and asked what she remembered of the meeting, she removed the cigar from her mouth only long enough to say, 'I won.'" When a reader of Hooper's account checked with Professor Anscombe about that, she answered on 10 October 1979, "The story is not true." ("Professor Anscombe Corrects Father Hooper," The *Canadian C. S. Lewis Journal*, December 1979, 7.)

12. "Dialogue," *Christianity & Literature* 28 (Fall 1978):9-11.
13. Royds Barfield, London attorney for the C. S. Lewis estate, sent me a signed letter dated 12 November 1980. The firm had advised its clients that there was very little doubt that certain allegations and implications I had made concerning the conduct of Walter Hooper (and Owen Barfield, by implication, as joint Trustee) were plainly defamatory. The two had so far declined to take legal action against me, but I was to understand that their patience was not inexhaustible.

    This stern warning referred to my questions about the bonfire story and the length of Hooper's tenure as Lewis's companion-secretary. I had not at that time questioned the authenticity of *The Dark Tower*. I first questioned *The Dark Tower* in my book *C. S. Lewis: Mere Christian* (third edition, 1987), pages 195-96 and 242—and no legal threats arrived from Royds Barfield or anyone else, I'm happy to say.
14. The nature of Hooper's scholarship may reflect a phenomenon described by theologian James M. Robinson: "The sociology of scholarship has been such as to reward those who get exclusive rights and then climb up the academic ladder with the status of those publishing important materials. In reality, they are not publishing it but blocking its publication." Quoted by John Dart in "Fragments from an Earthen Jar: James Robinson and the Nag Hammadi Library," *The Christian Century*, 1 March 1978, 214.

    Hooper has often referred to his Lewis papers that would be of great value to other Lewis researchers, but facts about Hooper's materials have come out extremely slowly and partially. Only Hooper knows exactly what he has. Furthermore, Lewis materials in the Wade Center and the Bodleian Library (donated by their owners) are available only to researchers who are physically able to study them there; they may not be photocopied or published unless the Estate gives permission. Hooper has sometimes denied to owners of even the most innocuous letters from C. S. Lewis the permission to make them public. (In 1979 Mrs. Harold Steed of Canada and in

1980 F. Morgan Roberts of the United States, a Presbyterian clergyman, were denied permission to make public their letters from C. S. Lewis. For details, see *The Canadian C. S. Lewis Journal*, August 1979, 5, and October 1980, 1.)

15. *Canadian C. S. Lewis Journal*, November 1979, 5.
16. A tape recorded personal interview with Leonard and Mollie Miller at their home in Eynsham on 27 December 1975.
17. Walter Hooper made this statement in a letter dated 27 June 1979, written in his "Lewisian script." The claim and relevant penmanship samples (not supporting the claim) were published on pages 8-9 of the April 1980 issue of the *Canadian C. S. Lewis Journal*.
18. C. S. Lewis, *Letters to an American Lady* (Grand Rapids, Mich.: Wm. B. Eerdmans Publishing Co., 1967), 120-21.
19. According to his entries in *Contemporary Authors* and *Crockford's Clerical Directory*, Hooper got his seminary training at St. Stephen's House, Oxford. Twice also that account has been given in articles about Hooper in his local newspaper, the *Greensboro Daily News*. The story there is that Hooper left his teaching post at the University of Kentucky to become Lewis's secretary in 1963; and after Lewis's death Hooper decided to study theology in England and become a priest. Although it is not often mentioned, Hooper attended Virginia Theological Seminary 1957-1959 but later had his name removed from the alumni roster. In the *Episcopal Clerical Directory* he did not list his theological training.
20. Hooper was admitted as a candidate for holy orders in the Diocese of North Carolina near the end of his seminary training, on 16 March 1959. He was dropped as a candidate on 8 September 1959. He was never ordained a priest in his home state of North Carolina. He was again admitted as a candidate for holy orders in September 1964, in the Diocese of Lexington, Kentucky, and was ordained a priest in June 1965. David Barrett's 1987 book *C. S. Lewis and His World* (Wm. B. Eerdmans and Marshall Pickering) is in error when it claims that Hooper was an American priest when he met C. S. Lewis in 1963.
21. Walter Hooper, "Introduction," in C. S. Lewis, *The Weight of Glory*, rev. ed. (New York: Macmillan, 1980), xi.
22. Sheldon Vanauken sent me a copy of these pages in 1980 or thereabouts, and I filed them. When I was working on this book I remembered them and asked if I could use them. Vanauken replied on 22 February 1987: "The interview was never published, and it's safe to conclude it never will be now. I just got it out and re-read it (it's all I have now, that fragment). I shall withhold the name of the interviewer; but yes, you may use it."
23. The three Lewis letters that Vanauken made public property are printed in appendix 2.
24. Wilfred Sheed, *The Good Word* (New York: Dutton, 1978), 3.
25. Jocelyn Gibb, *Light on C. S. Lewis* (New York: Harcourt, Brace & World, 1966).

26. This account moved Hooper's trip to England back seven years to 1956 and added a prestigious-sounding grant not mentioned anywhere else. In light of the information in note 8 above, it seems highly possible that this "grant" was the GI Bill.
27. This term used by Warren Lewis was made famous by Winston Churchill in a speech to the House of Commons on 22 February 1906.

THEY
FALL
TOGETHER

The two "C. S. Lewis secretaries," Major Warren Lewis and Walter Hooper, were supposedly good friends after C. S. Lewis's death. They were both bachelors who lived on in Oxford, both book-loving men, both devout Christians, and both passionately devoted to the memory of C. S. Lewis.

Neither Major Lewis nor Walter Hooper attended the small funeral of C. S. Lewis in his old churchyard on 26 November 1963; and neither one was eager to admit that fact afterwards. Warren Lewis did not attend because he was trying to drown his sorrow in alcohol, and Walter Hooper did not attend because he was living in Kentucky at the time.[1]

The death of C. S. Lewis absolutely shattered both men. There is no public account of how either of them got through the sad Christmas season after Lewis's death or how they first had any contact. But early in 1964 Hooper took a leave of absence from his teaching position at the University of Kentucky[2] and moved to a room in Oxford. The events that followed led to an angry climax that seems hard to believe.

As Hooper told the story over a decade later, by the end of January he had obtained a load of Lewis papers from the Kilns that gave him his future career as C. S. Lewis's editor, executor, trustee, estate manager, and literary advisor to the estate (the title has varied from time to time). That is Hooper's account of how he emerged from total anonymity at the time of Lewis's death to prominence through Lewis's book *Poems* less than a year later. It was in his introduction to *Poems* that Hooper introduced himself to Lewis readers as Lewis's companion- secretary. Lewis enthusiasts were completely surprised to learn of his existence and were eager to learn about Lewis from him.

As Hooper reminisced in *CSL*, bulletin of the New York C. S. Lewis Society in August 1977, his career began when he saved the poetry of C. S. Lewis from annihilation and then decided to publish it. Immediately after C. S. Lewis's death, Warren wanted to move into a smaller house in order to save money, and so he made the great three-day bonfire that Hooper called "the desecration."[3] One of the things Warren tossed out for burning was C. S. Lewis's most ardently prized possession, the blue notebook into which he had collected his poetry that he hoped to bring out in a book. Fortunately, Walter Hooper felt led to go to the Kilns and arrived on the scene in time to rescue the precious notebook from the flames.

Hooper has assured readers that he did not think Warren's intended annihilation of the blue notebook showed any lack of love toward his brother; it was just Warren's way of cleaning house.

Len and Mollie Miller, the household helpers, have said that it was not frugality that caused Warren Lewis to move out of the Kilns on 19 May 1964, so much as it was his nerves. He was so beset by impressions of his brother at every turn that he asked the Millers to locate him a house near theirs, which they did. They found him one on Ringwood Road, Headington. For months he slept there at night and spent most of his days at the Kilns, using two houses instead of one. He was extremely distraught.

"I again went to live with Major Lewis," is how Hooper states his own September move to 51 Ringwood Road (the word "again" is unexplained).[4] That month Warren wrote of his inability to get any information about his financial situation, his anxiety and desolation, and the fact that he had no one to chat with. In February of 1965 Warren wrote that one aspect of lonely old age he had not foreseen is boredom.[5] It is obvious that he was deeply depressed, and it is safe to assume that he tried to medicate himself with alcohol. Hooper's residence with Warren may have lasted eight months, and it was a painful period for everyone. According to Len Miller, the arrangement ended quite suddenly.

"I had to leave my old home in Headington Quarry and move into Oxford,"[6] Hooper wrote, accounting for his departure from Warren in the spring of 1965. By "my old home" Hooper refers to the Ringwood Road house in Headington (right next to Headington Quarry), where he had lived since September.

By this time Warren had suffered a minor stroke which left his right hand and his speech temporarily impaired.

He ended the year in Warneford Hospital, which he detested so much that he sometimes called it the Hellhole. On January 1 he wrote in his diary, "So begins a new year, and it is hard to imagine that it can be more miserable than 1965."[7] Indeed, Warren Lewis had no more years so miserable as 1965. Tracing the rest of his life, with the aid of his diary, reveals a story at times poignant, at times inspiring, at times delightful, and at times shocking. It is central to the C. S. Lewis hoax.

The Major's diary was a series of large blank books that he filled with his neat notes and essays and occasional illustrations of various kinds, such as clippings. His topics varied from his personal spiritual life and daily events to observations about his constant reading, news of interesting people, and nature descriptions. He liked to browse in his past volumes sometimes, and he noticed there the prominence of his three greatest pleasures in life: the company of C. S. Lewis, books, and scenery—in that order. Fourth would be dipping into the ocean, but he never got to do that often enough, so he didn't count it.

In his diary Warren described his typical day in 1966. From rising at 7:00 a.m. to retiring at 11:00 p.m. after a cup of Ovaltine, his days were methodical. They included prayers and Bible reading, breakfast, a morning walk, morning coffee with Mrs. Miller, lunch at 1:00 p.m. with the Millers, a drive with them or a nap after lunch, tea at 4:00, supper at 6:00, and television at the Miller home from 7:00 to 9:00. All the periods between these events were filled with reading books, Warren's main occupation.[8]

Fortunately, 1966 turned out much better than 1965. In April Warren was both glad and sorry about the advance copy of his own eighth book, *Letters of C. S. Lewis*, when it arrived from his publisher.[9] The book had been radically changed by other people, and he had not been given proofs to check before publication. Even his dedication had been cut out. His own version of the book had been titled *C. S. Lewis: A Biography* (the title later used by Green and Hooper for their book), and it had portrayed Lewis's life through selected passages from his letters, with transitions by Warren. It would have been a series of glimpses into Lewis's life a bit like the 1986 biography *C. S. Lewis: A Dramatic Life* by William Griffin. Changing his book into a traditional collection of letters made it far less appealing, in Warren's opinion. But he was pleased anyway.

On 16 June 1966, Warren turned seventy-one. His birthdays were always important to him. This time Len and Mollie Miller took him to Whipsnade Zoo, his first visit there since 1931 when he had gone with his brother (they had gone twice). He was delighted by the zoo. A week and a half later, on June 26, Clyde S. Kilby appeared at the Kilns to meet Warren, all the way from Wheaton, Illinois. Warren took a liking to him. A week later, the Millers and Warren Lewis took Dr. Kilby to see the Whipsnade Zoo, and Warren enjoyed the outing immensely.[10]

On August 19 the Millers and Warren took Dr. Kilby on another happy jaunt. Warren observed in his diary that the more one saw of Kilby, the more one realized the charming modesty and naivete at the root of his character. He noted that since Wheaton College was making a definitive collection of C. S. Lewis materials, he was adding a codicil to his will leaving all the Boxen materials from Lewis's childhood to Wheaton College.[11]

Less than two weeks later, Arthur Greeves died in his sleep in Ireland. Warren Lewis was deeply moved by the death of this lifelong acquaintance who had been a close friend of his brother's.

A few weeks after the death of Arthur Greeves, a Greeves relative mailed Warren a package that Greeves had addressed to him. Inside were 225 letters from C. S. Lewis to Greeves, spanning Lewis's life from 1914 to 1963. Warren decided to donate them to the collection at Wheaton College.

Christmas morning 1966 was perfect: bright, windless, with frost on all the puddles. But to Warren, and—he supposed—to most people his age, it was a sad day. He thought of the many Christmas mornings in all kinds of weather when he and C. S. Lewis had trudged off from the Kilns for the 8:00 a.m. communion service. Before the day was over, however, he had finished re-reading *All Hallow's Eve* by their old friend Charles Williams, and he found himself wondering aloud if Williams had been inspired by God when he wrote it. "Anyway, golly what a book!"[12]

Two days later Warren recorded an event that shows his benevolent alertness and good humor at the end of 1966. So far as he knew, the Blue Tit is the only bird addicted to cream. One in his neighborhood had discovered the milk bottles often left at Warren's door in the morning. On this morning the bird had not punched a hole in the foil cap with his beak, but had clipped all around the cap as neatly as a human could have done with scissors, "then made a hearty cream breakfast—which I did not grudge him."

Although every day of Warren's life after C. S. Lewis's death was dominated by the bereavement, he found happiness where he could. On 3 March 1967, Len Miller drove him to Malvern, where he enjoyed a weekend visit with George and Moira Sayer. On March 11 he began reading most of Shakespeare's plays, a spare-time project that he worked at for ten months. On April 17 he finally moved back into the Kilns, this time with Len and Mollie Miller agreeing to live there with him as family. In exchange for this kindness, they would receive a cheerful new house in Eynsham after he was gone, to be theirs until they both died.

According to the Millers, who were extremely fond of the Major, his drinking problem was mainly seasonal. On the anniversaries of a couple of tragic battles of the First World War, Warren would become morose and sink into a period of heavy drinking, more times than not. But he was a gentleman through and through, the finest of men. He battled his alcoholism year after year, with some successes and some failures. Their account of his character tallies exactly with the character of his diary entries.[13]

In 1969 Warren Lewis, who was a worrier in the first place, felt beset by insoluble problems. He was seventy-three years old and no doubt growing weary. His first bad news came in February, when word came to him in a roundabout way that Walter Hooper had written to Wheaton College saying that the Greeves letters belonged to the Bodleian Library of Oxford and must be returned. When the claim was not honored, Hooper reportedly suggested that a sister of Arthur Greeves, Lily Ewart, should be called in to decide between Wheaton and the Bodleian. Lily, Warren exclaimed, had about as much right to them as his house cat. All this about papers which were indisputably his property, the Major fumed, and given by him to Wheaton. He was furious.[14]

A few weeks later Warren and a close friend spent time discussing "a nightmare proposal" from Owen Barfield to make Hooper an executor of the Lewis literary estate.[15]

Warren was so upset about Hooper's "quite astonishing talent for *infiltration*" that he imagined that Hooper might try to move into the Kilns and take over his affairs. Furthermore, he worried that if Hooper started to come visiting as often as a couple of times a week (Hooper claims that he did so),[16] the Millers would dislike it and might move out. Warren got so excited about the whole matter that he thought he might do best to move away from Oxford. He wrote a vehement protest to Owen Barfield, but it did no good and Hooper was eventually appointed.

Warren's close friend (named in the diary) confided in Warren that personal papers belonging to C. S. Lewis had been taken from the Kilns without Warren's knowledge. The friend claimed he discussed the papers with Walter Hooper, who admitted he had taken them and claimed he had burned them. Warren felt all the more betrayed and helpless, as his diary shows.[17]

In May Warren learned that the London *Times* had identified Hooper as C. S. Lewis's secretary for "some years"; and when a friend wrote to correct that, she was told that Hooper's claim abated to a year at the Kilns with the two brothers. Warren was exasperated that the month of August was being expanded into the year of 1963 and that he was being included in the story.[18] He wrote a letter of protest to Hooper but did not think it would do any good. Indeed, in 1971, when Warren was still alive, Hooper would publish this sentence in *Imagination and the Spirit* (a collection of essays edited by Charles Huttar in honor of Clyde S. Kilby and published by Wm. B. Eerdmans):

> When I was living at The Kilns (his house in Oxford), Lewis was affectionately termed "The Boss"

by everyone there: his brother, secretary (myself), housekeeper, and gardener.[19]

Indeed, as late as 1987 a new book published simultaneously in England and the United States, C. S. *Lewis and His World* (Marshall Pickering and Wm. B. Eerdmans) featured Walter Hooper in the largest of many portraits in the book aside from one full-page portrait of C. S. Lewis. The bold-print caption identified Hooper thus: "Father Walter Hooper, who became Lewis's secretary in his last years."[20] That is almost twenty years after Warren and his friends tried in vain to stop the tale and eight years after the matter was aired in the *Los Angeles Times*. The fabrication that Warren detested has an uncanny survival record.

Another big worry of Warren's in 1969 was that Hooper was appointed to coauthor the official biography of C. S. Lewis along with Lewis's chosen biographer Roger Lancelyn Green. On July 25 Jock Gibb, the publisher, took Warren to lunch at Oxford's Randolph Hotel. Warren enjoyed the outing and was relieved to learn that Green would be the sole author of the book and that Hooper was only going to help with collection and arrangement of the material. Such assurance did not turn out to be true, as Warren no doubt realized eventually. Publication of the biography, however, was inexplicably delayed by Walter Hooper (according to Roger Lancelyn Green) until after Warren's death; so he never saw what it said.[21] It was just what he feared.

It seems likely that Warren Lewis (not to mention C. S. Lewis) would have snorted with irritation at Walter Hooper's interpolations of himself throughout the biography beginning with the year 1930. Before Hooper finally comes on the scene by visiting England (page 298), he has already appeared twenty-five times in the story in such insertions as "when Walter Hooper asked," "as Walter Hooper observed," "when Walter Hooper suggested," "as he told Walter Hooper," and even "When Walter Hooper met the Archbishop of Canterbury."[22]

In the last chapter, in the story of C. S. Lewis's life in 1963, the biography seems to indicate that Walter Hooper arrived in England in time to be a companion to C. S. Lewis throughout his last spring term at Cambridge.[23] That is an error. The claim that Hooper lived "as part of the household for several months later that year" is an error. And the indication that after Warren Lewis returned to Oxford in September, Walter Hooper left C. S. Lewis in late September is an error (he must have left earlier).[24]

There is an extremely curious passage by and about Hooper on page 303 of the biography. Hooper tells how once when he was out of the room, a visitor asked C. S. Lewis if he was not uncomfortable about having Hooper live in his house and intrude upon his private life. "But Walter is *part* of my private life!" Lewis shot back.

Hooper continues his account immediately:

> "Looking back, I find it hard to understand why Jack was so very kind to me," writes Hooper. "He was so vastly superior to me in every way that this fact—being known to *both* of us—may have made it easy to see me as a friend, perhaps, as he once said to Mrs. Miller, 'the son I should have had.'"

In those few lines, Hooper attributed to Lewis two statements about his own importance to Lewis—both said when Hooper was not in Lewis's presence and supposedly could not hear. When the biography was published, the person who heard the first statement was dead and could not be questioned. But Mrs. Miller was alive and denied that Lewis ever made the second statement.[25]

As a result of these peculiarities in the biography, most readers get the impression that Walter Hooper was central in the life of C. S. Lewis. This impression has spread widely because many writers have used the biography as a basic source of information. As *C. S. Lewis: A Biography* is summarized in *Masterplots 1974 Annual* (edited by Frank Magill and published by Salem Press in 1975), it is the biography of a famous twentieth- century scholar written by two close associates. The summary begins this way:

> *Principal personages:*
> C. S. Lewis, famous writer and scholar
> Joy Davidman Lewis, his wife
> Roger Lancelyn Green, writer and friend of Lewis
> The Reverend Walter Hooper, scholar and associate
>   of Lewis

Only four "personages" are mentioned. Warren Lewis is left out. And the writer of the summary can scarcely be faulted for the mistake.

It is painful to read in Warren's diary the record of his helpless fretting about Walter Hooper. He shuddered because he dreaded the statements Hooper might make after his death. He wrote that in his diary in so many words.

Apparently Warren's age, otherworldliness, sense of propriety, alcoholism, and heart trouble all conspired to make him impotent in Lewis affairs. But he was not totally impotent. He had an idea. He simply and quietly willed his diary to Wheaton College. When he died on 9 April 1973 (at the Kilns, reading a book), his whole story went to America, where he meant it to be read.[26]

Actually, when Dr. Kilby saw the distress about Walter Hooper in Warren Lewis's diary, he set it aside from the regular materials meant for general use there. He felt this matter required discretion and caution. Nevertheless, those who knew of the bad feeling between the Major and Walter Hooper could surmise that there would be unflattering references to Hooper in the Major's diary. They are indeed pithy. (When excerpts from the diary were published in 1982 by Harper & Row under the title *Brothers and Friends*, all references to Walter Hooper were deleted.)[27]

In 1974, one year after the Major's death, Walter Hooper published a fond tribute to him in *CSL*, the bulletin of the New York C. S. Lewis Society. "I was on intimate terms with him during the last ten years of his life," he stated.[28] Ironically, Hooper indicated twice in this tribute that he had lived with both brothers at the Kilns—the very claim that exasperated Warren beyond words.

With a kind of gallantry, Hooper avoided naming the Major's alcoholism as such ("I . . . feel that I should not write about [that] here"), but told the entertaining story that has, he said, passed into legend in Drogheda, Ireland. Once Mother Mary of the local hospital, in her late seventies, found Warren missing and drove her car to the White Horse pub; to the astonishment of everyone there, she walked into the bar, collected the heavy man, and carried him away.[29]

Within two years Walter Hooper's affectionate tone toward the Major had changed drastically. In 1979 Hooper published *They Stand Together: The Letters of C. S. Lewis to Arthur Greeves (1914-1963)*. This must be one of the strangest books of our century.

Walter Hooper has claimed that it took him ten years to edit the 296 letters to Greeves for publication. Since the letters were clearly written and in good order in the first place, and Hooper's competent footnotes are modest in number, the idea of a decade of editing is preposterous. One year would be generous for such a task. But that is the least preposterous of the strange features in this book.

The thirty-seven-page introduction by Walter Hooper culminates with an amazing attack upon Warren Lewis. To begin, Hooper claimed that Warren Lewis's dislike of Mrs. Moore first surfaced when Hooper was living with Warren, and it was scapegoating due to the misery caused by Warren's alcoholism. This flies in the face of Warren's diary entries decades earlier and C. S. Lewis's own words on the subject. On 18 April 1951, Lewis wrote to a Mrs. van Densen that he had lived most of his private life in a house full of senseless wranglings, lying, backbiting, follies, and *scares*. He had hardly ever gone home without terror about what might have happened next. Only now (after Mrs. Moore's recent death) did he begin to realize how bad it had been.[30]

There is rich irony in the fact that Hooper tells here how he and Owen Barfield wisely pressured Warren into removing his scathing criticism of Mrs. Moore from his introduction to Lewis's *Letters*,[31] in that this very introduction of Hooper's soon becomes a scathing attack upon Warren Lewis that apparently Hooper and Barfield agreed upon.

Hooper explained that when he met C. S. Lewis early in 1963 (he must have meant June, which is of course in the first half of 1963), Warren had already gone off on one of his binges.[32] At this point the story heats up.

C. S. Lewis had tried to be as generous as possible

with Warren, Hooper says, by making him the sole benefi-
ciary of the literary estate; but he had to appoint a couple
of friends as executors of that estate to prevent Warren
from "ending up in a ditch." This seems to hint that
Warren was not fully deserving of this inheritance and
that a worthier brother would not have warranted ap-
pointment of executors—both questionable assumptions.
What Hooper does not say is that Owen Barfield's legal
firm handled Lewis's business affairs all along; and when
Lewis died, Owen Barfield became literary executor, de-
legating responsibilities as he saw fit.

According to Hooper, C. S. Lewis used to lament,
"*Who* is there to look after him when I'm gone?"—refer-
ring to his brother. (I wonder where Hooper got this
quotation.) After C. S. Lewis's death, it occurred to
Walter Hooper that he should be the answer to C. S.
Lewis's lament.[33]

As Hooper tells it, he visited Warren every day in early
1964, and they usually had a pint or two of beer at the
local pub. But then Warren took his annual summer
vacation in Ireland, his homeland. Hooper says that Warren went there because the pubs rarely close there, and
also because the Oxford hospitals would no longer accept
him as an alcoholism patient; he had gone to them too
often. (Those two purported reasons raise questions of
their own, of course, but the matter is not worth pursuing
here.)

In Ireland Warren "roosted" in a hospital at night and
drank all day, Hooper says. Hooper joined Warren on 21
July 1964 and spent seven days pub-crawling with him.
Warren breakfasted on three triple gin-and-tonics and
then taxied from one pub to another all day, drinking a
triple-whiskey at each. Hooper does not make it clear if
he drank also, but he was trying to care for the Major.

All in all, Hooper spent four such vacations in Ireland with Warren, and he tells how they would get out of the taxi to see something and fall down into a hollow together. The story gets progressively worse.

On one trip the two were invited to a lovely inn for dinner, and the place was "full of high-ranking clerics and American tycoons." Warren had a few drinks and went to the restroom. Suddenly he bellowed, "Walter! Walter, come here!" Walter rushed in after him and found that Warren could not open his trousers because a well-meaning nun had put them on him backwards that morning. So Hooper saved the drunken Major from disaster in the restroom. Warren's behavior was so draining that the Drogheda hospital had to tell him not to return.

Back in Oxford, Warren would sit in his study chair for as long as two weeks at a time without getting up for anything, eating nothing, drinking as much as six bottles of whiskey a day (this is Hooper's exact claim on page 34). Perhaps this should all go into the *Guinness Book of World Records* .

Because Warren could not tell day from night, he called for Hooper's services at any time. As a result, Hooper spent more than a year without one night of uninterrupted sleep. (This year must have been squeezed into the eight months when the two men lived together.) Not even then, he remarked, could he bear Warren any bad will. Hooper suffered so much that he had to recognize how selfish Warren was, but he loved him anyway.

Later, when Warren was living with the Millers back at the Kilns, he was sober more often. All that Hooper had gone through with Warren seemed worth it when Hooper spent some of the most pleasant days in his memory at the Kilns then. The Millers and the Major and Hooper made a "family" of four who had many happy times together before Warren died in 1973.

But long before those happy latter days, a scandalous event had occurred, which Hooper recounts for us in his Editor's Note following his Introduction. On a dank morning in November of 1966, Hooper arrived on his daily visit to the Major at Ringwood Road to tend to his needs. (This was the month before the Blue Tit got into the cream by the front door, and in his diary the Major seems lucid and competent. He does not mention Hooper's daily visits to take care of him.) There was a good fire in the grate. On this day a registered parcel and letter arrived from Belfast, and Hooper had to help Warren by opening them. The parcel contained the 225 C. S. Lewis letters to Greeves. Lily Ewart, a sister of Greeves, had sent along a letter asking Warren to deliver these letters to the Bodleian for Arthur. (Arthur had no particular interest in the Bodleian Library, and so his decision not to give the letters to Warren seems rather surprising.)

Hooper read Lily's letter aloud to the inattentive Warren so many times that he was able to memorize part of it and, fortunately, happened to write it down in his diary that day. That sounds almost too fortunate to be true; it also sounds unnecessary. Arthur was dead, but Lily was alive. She was perfectly capable of repeating her message and making sure that Arthur's intentions had been carried out. But apparently neither Warren nor Hooper considered that fact at the time or later.

That very morning, Warren destroyed the letter and seized the Greeves collection that had been entrusted to him. He pretended that Arthur had given the letters to him (Lily Ewart could have contested that if she had heard about it), and sent the bundle to Wheaton College. Naturally, the trustees (Walter Hooper and Owen Barfield) later notified both the Bodleian and Wheaton that the 225 Lewis letters had been confiscated by Warren on their way to the Bodleian. But Wheaton disagreed.

Hooper cites Lily Ewart as his one witness that Arthur had intended for Warren to place the set of letters in the Bodleian Library, and he cites his own diary entry as proof. But Lily Ewart was alive for ten years after she purportedly wrote her letter to Warren Lewis and he purportedly destroyed it. Unfortunately, Lily Ewart died in 1976, and Walter Hooper did not tell about her letter that Warren destroyed until 1979; so no one could contact Lily Ewart about her claims that survive now only in Walter Hooper's diary.

Actually, because of a letter-exchange agreement, photocopies of all the Greeves letters were in the Bodleian Library anyway. (When fifty more letters from Lewis to Arthur Greeves were donated to the Bodleian Library, by way of Walter Hooper, they were kept "under seal" and the Bodleian was not allowed to send copies to Wheaton until after *They Stand Together* was published. The reason, according to Hooper, was "We didn't want to act precipitately." The delay was inexplicable and could raise questions about the authenticity of the letters, especially the key letter dated 30 October 1955, which Hooper cites as evidence that the Lewis marriage was never consummated.)[34]

There is a major difference between the original letters to Greeves and the photocopies, and that may be why the trustees especially wanted easy access to the originals. Some passages in the letters were blotted out in later years because they were about embarrassing sexual topics that the two letter-writers did not want others to know about. But modern technology can retrieve such censored passages.

As Hooper states the matter, it is one of life's most pleasant comedies to see elderly people embarrassed by things from their younger years (Hooper does not mention where he got such a notion of pleasant comedy). It was charming of Arthur Greeves, idling before his death, to try to make Lewis's letters more "respectable." According to Hooper, this was an earthly grace of Arthur's that balanced C. S. Lewis's high-flown intellect. Hooper felt it was his role as manager of Lewis's estate to publish the letters as written in spite of the intentions of Lewis and Greeves.

Therefore, Bob O'Donnell and David Elders of Lord and King Associates (the Illinois producer of *Through Joy and Beyond*) went to Wheaton College for Walter Hooper and photographed the "deleted passages" with infra-red and ultra-violet fluorescence photography. (It is assumed their findings were correct; oddly enough, no one has ever checked.)

The "deleted passages," which refer to Arthur Greeves's attraction to young boys (he never married) and C. S. Lewis's attraction to sado-masochism, are set off in the text of the book by ‹pointed brackets› so that they are easy to locate. Those who consider this tasteless are apt to stand accused of sharing Arthur Greeves's misguided sense of propriety.

But at one point Walter Hooper himself displays a surprising sense of delicacy. When giving C. S. Lewis's reasons for disliking Malvern College, on page 10 of this very introduction, Hooper daintily omits what Lewis saw as pervasive preoccupation with homosexual relationships among his fellow students there. Lewis wrote of this frankly, openly, and very negatively in his autobiography; but Hooper skips it.[35] Conservative readers might wish Hooper had skipped the allure of pederasty and sado-masochism instead.

The extraordinary book introduction ends with Hooper's usual thanks and acknowledgments that are almost courtly in their grace. For example, he links Owen Barfield to his title: "Lewis's finest legacy to me—my friend Owen Barfield has stood by me all the way."

Anthony Marchington had a hand in this book also. "I am fortunate beyond all covenant," Hooper vowed, "in living in the same house and being helped so much by Anthony Marchington who is, as Lewis said of one of his contemporaries, 'the sole Horatio known to me in this age of Hamlets.'"

This all sounds very serious; but Anthony Marchington was the author of the Lewis Bonfire hoax-letter, and things are not always as serious as they seem.

The original edition of this book was a Collins hardback with a burnt-orange dustjacket. The inside back flap of the jacket presented the following information about Walter Hooper:

> Hooper discovered the works of C. S. Lewis just on the point of entering the army in 1954, and so totally smitten was he by Lewis that he went through basic training with a rifle in one hand and a copy of Lewis's *Miracles* in the other. He began corresponding with C. S. Lewis in 1954. After leaving the army he read theology and soon took up a post at the University of Kentucky lecturing on Medieval and Renaissance English literature. After some years there he received an invitation from Lewis to visit him in Oxford, and he took a leave of absence for the simple but to him, very significant pleasure of spending an afternoon with Lewis. What was ex-

pected to be a simple tea party has lasted fifteen years. A week after they met in the spring of 1963 Lewis asked Hooper to remain in Oxford as his companion-secretary, which position Hooper was more than delighted to accept. Their friendship grew to the point that Lewis called him "the son I should have had."

This passage obviously has a few problems in it. Although Hooper has often referred to his decade of letters from C. S. Lewis, and has persuaded people to donate their own original Lewis collections to the Bodleian Library, he has not yet donated even photocopies of his own collection to the Bodleian. In January 1980, the *Canadian C. S. Lewis Journal* questioned whether his collection really exists.[36]

"Some years" as a lecturer on Medieval and Renaissance literature (Lewis's specialty) seems impossible on two counts. Hooper was at the University of Kentucky only five semesters, and he was an entry-level instructor, not a professor. According to Dr. Robert O. Evans, the primary medievalist at that time was Dr. Arthur K. Moore, followed by Dr. Steve Manning. This subject was not taught by beginners.[37]

It is impossible to believe that Lewis would ask anyone to travel across the ocean just to have tea with him, aside from the fact that Hooper was reportedly there already to attend summer school. Hooper didn't take a leave of absence from Kentucky until two months after Lewis's death. According to most of Hooper's own accounts, it was during Lewis's mental derangement in mid-July when Lewis asked Hooper to help with correspondence, not in June. Hooper did not remain in England as Lewis's secretary, and no one claims to have heard Lewis call Hooper "the son I should have had."

Aside from these matters, the introduction can stand.

Of course book jackets are not noted for their accuracy. They often include some inaccuracy or exaggeration. The inside front flap of *They Stand Together* indulges in hyperbole:

> This work, which was ten years in preparation, is clearly the finest piece of scholarship ever done on the writings of C. S. Lewis . . . the wit, the Christian apologetics, and, in some letters hitherto under seal, the heart-break of seeing an older brother slither into tragic alcoholism. . . . With this volume Walter Hooper has taken a laurel which few will share.

The contrast between Walter Hooper winning a laurel and Warren Lewis "slithering" into alcoholism, as well as "roosting" in a hotel, is remarkable. One can imagine how C. S. Lewis would feel. (Warren's alcoholism caused both brothers much pain, and C. S. Lewis sometimes complained bitterly in private. But he would have been horrified at a public attack upon Warren.)

Alert readers of *They Stand Together* were apt to notice something odd about the front cover of the book in the first place. It features handsome photos of the young Lewis and the young Greeves, both set in ovals. They are flanking a sketch of Oxford's Magdalen Tower, which thrusts up between them. That seems an illogical symbol of the friendship, since the tower was a key landmark in Lewis's academic life but had nothing at all to do with Greeves, who lived indolently in Ireland and never even attended a university (he attended Slade School of Art briefly). The common passion of the two men for rural Irish scenery could have provided a more appropriate symbol, and one that did not happen to strongly resemble a design often used in the homosexual subculture in various guises.

But the really odd part of the cover is the title. *They Stand Together* happens to be a little-known homosexual euphemism on both sides of the Atlantic.[38]

Of course it may be that no one who was involved with the book production knew that this title is a little inside joke. But the fact is that about seven years after the listing of the book everywhere and its wide acceptance and good sales, the title was suddenly dropped. The book is now sold without any sign of the original cover design and without the words "They Stand Together" on the cover. It now goes by its subtitle, *The Letters of C. S. Lewis to Arthur Greeves (1914-1963)*. Titles aren't usually dropped that way.

Somewhere, Screwtape or someone else must still be laughing about the original cover. But C. S. Lewis and Warren Lewis would not appreciate the joke.

Another rather sad joke on Warren Lewis is that among his 1969 frustrations, one was the rejection of Boxen. He had expected Jock Gibb (of the Geoffrey Bles company) to publish his beloved collection of C. S. Lewis's childhood writing and drawing. But on 25 July 1969, Gibb broke the news at lunch that they were putting the Boxonian Saga "on ice" because several at the firm thought it might accidentally be regarded by the public as the origin of Narnia. Warren could see that this objection did not make any sense at all and that there must be a different, unspoken reason for the rejection.

Four months later, Warren enjoyed a visit from Roger Lancelyn Green, who told him that trustee Owen Barfield objected to publication of Boxen because the stories are not interesting and have no literary merit. Barfield was in charge of the literary estate. Warren Lewis fully owned the materials themselves, but that did not give him the power to publish them. It seems a bit sad that people who were profiting handsomely from Lewis's literary estate did not see fit to add some warmth to Warren Lewis's last three years by humoring him with a small printing of his beloved Boxen. Warren innocently believed it would never be published.[39]

In January 1972, Warren had a pacemaker installed. He did not feel well that year, but in June he enjoyed a visit from a professional photographer from the United States, Douglas R. Gilbert. Gilbert came to the Kilns to take pictures of the Major's memorabilia, some of which would appear in *C. S. Lewis: Images of His World*. Clyde Kilby told me that Warren used to keep these Lewis family papers locked in a drawer in his bedroom for safety. Gilbert says he laid out the books, notebooks, and papers on the rug of the Kilns and photographed them there. He still has the negatives and proofs because he keeps all his photography projects.[40] One can see the rug behind the objects in the pictures.

Two months after Gilbert's photography session, in August, Warren Lewis went to Ireland for a visit. There his health worsened, and he had to stay all winter. Leonard and Mollie Miller took care of the Kilns and the Major's business, and Leonard Miller flew to Ireland to visit Warren there several days every month.[41]

Early in April 1973, Warren Lewis finally returned home to Oxford and died in the Kilns on April 9. The Millers instantly notified a courier appointed in advance by Clyde Kilby to pick up Warren's irreplaceable diary and other family papers from his bedroom on the day of his death. The plan seemed to work. Thus, less than one year after Douglas Gilbert went to the Kilns to photograph Warren Lewis's personal collection, the collection was sent to the Wade Center in Illinois, according to Warren's will. Gilbert could have stayed home and photographed it there.

But Gilbert would have missed a few of his photographs if he had waited, because some of what the Major showed him never went to Illinois. Apparently certain childhood Lewis notebooks disappeared from the Kilns between June 1972 and April 1973. Then in 1985 Walter Hooper published his book *Boxen*, including some material from those very notebooks. Hooper said he had received two of the childhood notebooks as a gift from C. S. Lewis in 1963 and had rescued two more from the Lewis bonfire in 1964. (For a detailed analysis of *Boxen* and other Lewis juvenilia, see appendix 1, "Stealing the King's Ring.")

Perhaps someone will come up with an explanation eventually, but so far there hasn't been any. There are several other peculiarities about Hooper's *Boxen* besides the missing notebooks. For example, I am sure the skillful "King's Ring" drawings attributed by Hooper to six-year-old C. S. Lewis were really by an adult in the Lewis household, and the "King's Ring" drawing really done by six-year-old Lewis was left out of Hooper's *Boxen* because it is too childish (Gilbert has a photo of it, and I have a copy). The final piece in Hooper's *Boxen*, a turgid essay called "Encyclopedia Boxoniana" (saved from the Lewis bonfire), was purportedly written by Lewis when he was a young Oxford professor. It seems to me to be from the same amateurish hand that wrote *The Dark Tower* and "The Man Born Blind."

Indeed, we are all "born blind" on this subject of C. S. Lewis affairs. We are groping, and we are slow to be able to see what's going on. As Mollie Miller remarked affectionately about Warren Lewis, "He was a bit simple, you know." I think we all are a bit simple—those who hoax others, as well as those who are hoaxed. We might as well accept the fact in good spirit.

"It is almost always worth while to be cheated; people's little frauds have an interest which more than repays what they cost us." Logan Pearsall Smith made that claim in 1931 in *Afterthoughts*. Smith may have been exaggerating the entertainment value of hoaxes, but he had a point. We tend to be fascinated by fraud.

Perhaps this is because of our deep spiritual longing to be ultimately uncheated and undeceived. Much of human life itself is deceptive, and our final enemy is the confidence artist called Death. C. S. Lewis and his brother are now laughing at that cheater, I think. And at all the other pain and loss and defeat that hoaxed them here on earth.

Where they are now, only reality exists.

Chapter 8, Notes

1. William Griffin, on page xxv of his book C. S. *Lewis: A Dramatic Life*, said that he was at the funeral "albeit figuratively." In that unusual sense both Warren Lewis and Walter Hooper were there also, no doubt, with thousands of others.
2. Lewis W. Cochran, Vice-President of Academic Affairs at the University of Kentucky, says that Walter Hooper was employed as a full-time instructor in the then department of English, speech, and dramatic arts, and resigned effective 31 January 1964. This information is in the faculty records and appears on page 7 of the January 1980 *Canadian C. S. Lewis Journal*. According to notes in the University archives, Hooper was probably on leave of absence from 1964 to 1966.
3. Hooper used the term *desecration* on page 42 of his "Introduction" for *They Stand Together* (London: Collins, 1979).
4. Walter Hooper, "Reflections of an Editor," CSL: *The Bulletin of the New York C. S. Lewis Society*, August 1977, 3.
5. *Brothers and Friends: The Diaries of Major Warren Hamilton Lewis*, ed. Clyde S. Kilby and Marjorie Lamp Mead (San Francisco: Harper and Row, 1982), 254.
6. Hooper, "Reflections," 4.
7. *Brothers and Friends*, 255.
8. Ibid., 257.
9. Ibid., 256-57.

10. Ibid., 260-62.
11. Ibid., 265-66.
12. Ibid., 267.
13. The Millers expressed this view of Warren Lewis in an interview on 27 December 1975 at their home in Eynsham.
14. On 8 February 1969, Warren Lewis recorded in his diary the lunch he had with Glenn Sadler, a graduate of Wheaton College and friend of Clyde Kilby: ". . . disclosure of yet another of Walter's Jesuitical maneuvers. It appears he has now written to Clyde saying that Jack's letters to Arthur are merely on loan to Wheaton, being the property of the Bodleian's where they must sooner or later be returned—which is untrue. Apparently there must have been a demur from Clyde met by Walter with the suggestion that Lily Ewart of all people should be called in to decide whether Bodleian or Wheaton is the owner of the letters! Lily, who has almost as much right in them as has Jan, our house cat! And all this about letters which were beyond dispute my property and given by me to Wheaton. In his tireless, unscrupulous busybodyness Walter is the perfect Jesuit." Thinking that Sadler or Warren Lewis could have been mistaken about the matter, I checked with Kilby, and he told me it was all true.
15. Major Warren Lewis's diary entry on 10 March 1969: "[Name withheld] came up in time for supper last night and stopped until this morning as a preliminary to making one of a claret tasting committee at Balliol, and an enjoyable visit it has been. It would have been even more so if we had not had to waste so much time discussing the blocking of a nightmare proposal from Owen Barfield that Walter Hooper should be appointed heir apparent to an Executor's position. Apparently he has had the impudence to tell Owen that such a suggestion is approved by me! [Name withheld] I'm glad to say, is as emphatically opposed to the idea as I am myself, and we roughed out letters of protest which we were to send to Owen, I posting mine via [name withheld] this morning. He has even stronger views on Master Walter than I have, and distrusts him absolutely . . . Leaving aside the amazing impudence of this theft I'm cetain (a) wherever he found the papers it was not in the spare room and (b) that in view of their contents he so far from destroying them, has hidden them away to be published as soon as it is safe to do so. Which cannot be in my lifetime thank God! I begin to be very tired of Walter's pranks. He has a brazen impudence exceeding that of Ponsonby Staples but deriving from the Staples school . . . What can ordinary civil people do with such a man?"
16. "I was to see Major Lewis very frequently—usually once or twice a week—for the rest of his life." Hooper stated this on page 4 of "Reflections of an Editor." On 26 October 1977, Leonard Miller responded to that in a letter, "Walter certainly didn't visit him as often as he says."
17. Someone who was concerned about these matters actually showed me the Major's diaries in 1974 and gave me photocopies of a few pages, without the knowledge of Curator Clyde Kilby. Shortly after that, the rapidly expanding Lewis collection was relocated in new facilities, and the diaries were more carefully guarded during the rest of Clyde Kilby's tenure. Fol-

lowing the publication of *Brothers and Friends* and Kilby's retirement, however, there was a quiet shift in policy, and now researchers at the Wade Center may examine the diaries if they want to do so. However, because the diaries are voluminous and only recently open to the public, few researchers have made use of them so far. The writing in the diaries belongs to the Wade Center, and Lyle Dorsett is willing to consider publishing more excerpts from the diaries in volumes to supplement *Brothers and Friends*, if a publisher were willing.

18. Warren Lewis's diary entry, 12 May 1969: "I'm in further trouble about Walter. Jean wrote to the Times protesting against their statement that he had been Jack's secretary for "some years" before J's death and has now had a reply from the Editor to say that Jock Gibb "sticks to his guns" and that they have been in touch with Walter himself, whose claim has now abated to "a year." But he then made the astonishingly impudent assertion that he had "lived in" with J. and me here whilst so doing. This is simply untrue. I never met him until after J's death, and Mollie, whose memory is to be trusted in such matters assures me, as does Len, that the period for which he forced himself on poor J. was the month of August 1963! I'm afraid there is no way of blinking the fact that in his frantic endeavors to put himself over as one of J's oldest and most intimate friends he has now been guilty of a couple of what are called in Parliament "terminological inexactitudes." I've written to him of course, but he has a front of brass and will no doubt continue to present his false image to the public—and what can I do? I dread the statements he may make after my death in the book, which he will have the skill to make with seeming authority. I wish J. had never met him."

19. Walter Hooper, "Past Watchful Dragons: The Fairy Tales of C. S. Lewis" in *Imagination and the Spirit: Essays in Literature and the Christian Faith Presented to Clyde S. Kilby*, ed. Charles A. Huttar (Grand Rapids, Mich.: Wm. B. Eerdmans Publishing Co., 1971), 286.

20. David Barrett, *C.S. Lewis and His World* (Grand Rapids, Mich.: Wm. B. Eerdmans Publishing Co., 1987), 43.

21. On 29 December 1970 Walter Hooper wrote to me that he expected to finish the Lewis biography in the summer of 1971. On 7 October 1971, he wrote to me that he was still at work on the biography. On 8 November 1972 he wrote to me that he still had three chapters of the biography left to write. Finally, on 3 February 1973, he wrote that the biography was finished and in the hands of the publisher. It was then released in 1974.

When I interviewed Roger Lancelyn Green at his ancestral home, Poulton Hall at Poulton-Lancelyn near Cheshire on 1 January 1975, I asked him what had caused the delay between 1971 and 1973. He told me the long delay was still a mystery to him and had been quite a frustrating experience. Green said he had to go ahead and write most of the book himself while waiting for Hooper to join him on the project. Green wrote chapters 1, 2, 3, 6, 7, and 10, plus material that had to be cut out because of the book's excess length; after Hooper received Green's chapters, he filled in later with chapters 4, 5, 8, and 9—plus an account in chapter 10 of his own role in Lewis's life. It took Hooper four years to produce those four chapters, Green observed, and Hooper never explained the delay to Green.

Because I wanted to be sure that there was no possibility of my misunderstanding Green or remembering wrong, I wrote and asked him to repeat what he had told me about coauthoring the biography. His answer was delayed by illness that interfered with his handwriting; the illness was later diagnosed as Parkinson's disease, which forced him to depend upon his son Richard Lancelyn Green to be his scribe near the end of his life. In a neat but laboriously written letter to me dated 1 March 1978, Green repeated his outline of the composition of the biography, including the fact that it took Hooper four years to produce his four chapters.

22. To me it seems obvious that these insertions are in the style of Walter Hooper, not the style of Roger Lancelyn Green, and that many of them are things Green would not have known about.

23. Green said in his letter of 1 March 1978 that the material about Hooper in the last chapter was by Hooper.

24. Warren Lewis insisted that he never met Walter Hooper in 1963, and the Millers agreed. It seems clear that Hooper could not have been living at the Kilns when Warren was there in 1963. Furthermore, C. S. Lewis wrote to an American correspondent on 30 August 1963 that Warren was not home yet and so he had no secretarial help at all (*Letters to an American Lady* [Grand Rapids, Mich.: Wm. B. Eerdmans Publishing Co., 1967], 121). This tallies with the fact that Hooper was teaching in Kentucky in September 1963.

25. Personal interview with Leonard and Mollie Miller in Eynsham on 27 December 1975. Mrs. Miller hotly denied the Lewis quotation wrongly attributed to her.

26. According to the footnote on p. 266 of *Brothers and Friends*, Warren Lewis carefully reviewed all materials he willed to the Wade Center, excising only one page of his diaries. He enjoyed reading published diaries, and he had a strong conviction that diaries should be preserved and read.

27. The editorial note on p. xxviii of *Brothers and Friends* explains, "It should also be noted that certain passages in this manuscript were deleted at the request of and as a courtesy to the C. S. Lewis Estate." Trustees of the Estate at that time were the fifty-one-year-old Walter Hooper and eighty-four-year-old Owen Barfield. They had no legal control over publication of Major Warren Lewis's diary, but their desire for deletions somehow prevailed before the book went to press.

28. Walter Hooper, "Warren Hamilton Lewis: An Appreciation," CSL, April 1974, 5-8.

29. Ibid.

30. Lewis's exact words are quoted by Warren Lewis in *Brothers and Friends*, 265.

31. *They Stand Together*, 23.

32. Ibid., 30.

33. Hooper has also quoted similar helpless lamenting by Warren Lewis after C. S. Lewis's death: "'What, oh *what*,' he groaned, 'would Jack think if he saw me being carried off to the work-house?'" This was published in

Hooper's article "Warren Hamilton Lewis: An Appreciation," 7. In a letter dated 29 November 1977, Leonard Miller responded doubtfully, "I don't think the Major would have said that about the workhouse. . . . As for the mental state of the Major, he certainly was an alcoholic. But this did nothing to make him a lunatic as some people are trying to make out. Have you read any of the Major's books?"

34. In *They Stand Together* Hooper attached to this letter a three-and-a-half page footnote essay explaining away the Lewis "marriage." (The quotation marks are Hooper's.)

35. Another interesting kind of delicacy on Hooper's part showed up in a letter to me dated 9 December 1977, where he twice changed the x to q and spelled *homosexuality* as *homosequality*. He has clear handwriting and ordinarily appears to be an excellent speller. I have no other examples of Hooper's spelling of this particular word. I had asked him for Lewis's attitude toward practicing homosexuals, and Hooper's answer was clear and reasonable except for the playful spelling.

36. Although he claims to own a decade of letters from Lewis, the only passage that Hooper has published is a brief one from a letter dated 11 October 1963, all about Hooper. (This appears on page 31 of *They Stand Together*.) The selection ends, "Your absence makes a cavity like a drawn tooth!" Because the Millers claimed that Lewis was satisfied with Hooper's absence, this quotation needs to be examined and verified as genuine Lewis. In any case, this is an odd figure of speech to use with a new friend who is absent and planning to be back in four months.

37. In a letter dated 3 November 1987, Dr. Evans stated, "I can say this much: Hooper was never a professor at UK. . . . He certainly did not teach medieval lit."

38. I have been informed of this underground use of the term by one English person and one American, without my asking for the information. Since then an American affirmed that use of the term when asked. However, I have not yet located anyone willing to be cited on the topic in a footnote.

39. Warren agreed to let Green borrow the Lewis family papers, and this is how he noted that in his diary entry for 26 November 1969:

"Roger Green turned up soon after twelve thirty as per agreement and left for London at 2:15. It was an enjoyable break for me, and we had some good crack. Rather against my better judgment I consented to let him borrow the complete Lewis Papers when he is ready to make use of them for the life; it would have been churlish to refuse him, yet I shrink from letting such a treasured and irreplaceable collection out of my own keeping. . . . I look forward to his coming down for the night to discuss the book with me some time next year."

40. Letters from Douglas R. Gilbert to me, 10 November 1986 and 4 June 1987.

41. Leonard Miller described this period and what he saw as chronic misman-agement of the business affairs of the Lewis brothers in the tape recording made at the Miller home in Eynsham, England, on 27 December 1975.

Appendix 1

STEALING
THE KING'S
RING

Note to the reader. In an earlier draft of this book, "Stealing the King's Ring" appeared as chapter 9. But Roger Lancelyn Green advised me to drop chapter 9 because chapter 8 had more impact and made a better ending. When my editor made the same suggestion, I saw that Green was right. The truth about the juvenilia is set forth here in an appendix for readers curious enough to explore these facts.

Clumsy stories about Sir Peter Mouse and the history of Animal-land are beneath the notice of most adults, even if the author and illustrator was a little boy named Clive Staples Lewis. But since almost anything written by C. S. Lewis has sold prodigiously during the first twenty-five years after his death, a hardback book called *Boxen: The Imaginary World of the Young C. S. Lewis* was published in 1985 and soon spread all over England and the United States. Store managers wondered whether to place it with books for children, religious books, biography, or adult fiction. Perhaps it belongs in the mystery section instead.

Like *The Dark Tower*, part of C. S. Lewis's childhood art and writing was almost cast into Major Lewis's catastrophic three-day bonfire in his orchard in January, 1964. (Chapter 2 explored the likelihood that this famous bonfire never took place.) Editor Walter Hooper tells again about this close call in his introduction to *Boxen*: how on the third day of the bonfire Lewis's gardener Fred Paxford asked to be allowed to save some of the papers for Hooper, and how Major Lewis answered (unreasonably) that the papers had to be burned unless Hooper happened to visit that very day. Fortunately, Hooper was led to come and rescue many things from the flames, including a notebook and an exercise book full of Lewis juvenilia.

Hooper added this material to the two notebooks of Lewis juvenilia that he had already received as a personal gift from C. S. Lewis six months earlier, when he was visiting Oxford in the summer of 1963. Apparently Hooper means for us to assume that he took the first two gift notebooks home to Kentucky with him in early September and then brought them back to England in January, 1964, and kept them secret—in his own words, "most tenderly preserved." It was right after this return to England when Hooper met Major Warren Lewis for the first time and then obtained more of the early juvenilia out in the orchard.

Hooper has not seemed to notice what a remarkable coincidence it is that after the Lewis brothers had cherished their childhood material for over fifty years, a brand new friend obtained much of it within six months, through two entirely unrelated events. This is all the more remarkable in light of the fact that he was in the United States most of that six-month period. It seems that Warren Lewis, who took immense interest in the juvenilia and some interest in life's coincidences, was apparently unaware that Hooper had acquired either set of the early material.

Even when Hooper coauthored the 1974 volume *C. S. Lewis: A Biography*, he was not yet ready to tell coauthor Green or the public about his private collection of Lewis's childhood productions. According to that official biography, only a few poems—not any stories—survived from Lewis's Animal-land.[1] That is what Green sincerely believed at the time.

The biography was wrong about all Animal-land stories being lost. Hooper's personal collection of Animal-land prose is at least as interesting as the set of longer products from Lewis's later childhood which are not about Animal-land, but the land of Boxen. (All of Lewis's juvenilia is commonly referred to as Boxen material, whether it is early or late and refers to Animal-land or Boxen. Hence the book title *Boxen* for a book which includes a variety of childhood materials.)

Although the Lewis brothers had probably lost or discarded some of their juvenilia through the years, and had long ago sentimentally buried in the garden the toys that inspired the stories, Warren Lewis was carefully preserving most of it in a locked drawer in his bedroom toward the end of his life. He was a bit concerned about its safety. He had willed it to the Marion E. Wade Center in Wheaton, Illinois, and it went there when he died in 1973. A decade later, the Wade Center gave Walter Hooper free use of the Wade's juvenilia for his 1985 volume *Boxen*, and his position with the Lewis estate gave him the legal right to publish it. So he did. And he presented it with great scholarly flourish, showing how he valued it.

Hooper has arranged the materials in *Boxen* chronologically, which meant starting with the material in his private collection rather than the Wade material. *Boxen* begins with a three-act play titled "The King's Ring," probably written when Lewis was seven years old. Whether one finds it a valuable example of creativity from an unusual child or no more than early practice from an author who became interesting later, some familiarity with it is needed in order to grasp the puzzles involved in *Boxen*.

The play begins with this first scene:

KING BUNNY: This wine is good.
BAR-MAN: I shall drink a stiff goblet to the health
            of King Bunny.
KING BUNNY: For the good toast much thanks.
SIR PETER: Draws near the dinner hour so pleas
            your Magasty.

In the second scene the mouse named Hit, who had been the bar-man, visited the King in Pip Castle and tricked him into taking off his ring. Hit disappeared with the ring.

In the third scene Sir Peter announced to some of King Bunny's retinue that the ring was lost. Immediately thereafter, Hit entered and sold the ring to one of the King's friends. Hit had disguised the ring so it would not be recognized.

In the second act, Hit had shot one of King Bunny's musicians with an arrow and had fled to Cannon-Town. The King and his friends went to Cannon-town and dubbed Hit a knight in order to get to know him better, because he was their prime suspect.

In the third act, the frog named Mr. Big recognized the disguised ring of the King on the hand of a friend and accused him of being the thief. Sir Peter exclaimed, "Who!! Which!! Where!! When!! Why!! How!!" Then wise Sir Goose explained Hit's trickery. Soon Sir Goose captured Hit. The King received his lost ring back and prepared to sail home. The play ends.

KING BUNNY: Now I think we must go back to
Mouse-land. Look the sun hath clove the earth in
2. *

(Curtain.)

THE END

* The anchient Mice believed that at sun-set the sun cut a
hole in the earth for its self.

This simple play has a large cast of characters, and
the child Lewis's own cast-of-characters page is reproduced in the book in all its ink-blotted glory, a clumsy
and extremely ambitious list for a seven-year-old boy, in
both printing and cursive script. It was tidied up a bit in
the printed version (Icthus-oress for ic-this-oress, General
for generel), but much of the eccentricity is preserved,
apparently at random.

Most Lewis enthusiasts would have preferred many
more facsimile pages in *Boxen* and photos of the old
notebooks Lewis used and treasured. The more interested
one is in children's art and writing, the more questions
one has that *Boxen*, in its present format, does not answer.
For example, there is no hint about the size of Lewis's
illustrations or, in many cases, their location. Scale is
one of the factors in the charm of juvenilia. There is no
word about the size and length of the notebooks or the
number of pages devoted to a given project. Readers have
no way to get a sense of proportion or position for the
materials.

Of course readers assume that the four ink drawings
illustrating "The King's Ring" are by Lewis and that they
are all we have of his illustrations for the project. They
are wonderful for a seven-year-old boy. Not only is the
perspective and composition advanced, but the boldness,

accuracy, and vitality of the ink drawing is amazing in contrast to his immature printing. Most notable are the figures. King Bunny, various mice, and the Golliwog are charming creatures depicting actual toys in the Lewis nursery. In some scenes the plump mice, clad only in fur and whiskers, perch on their haunches in genuinely mousy style. Few adults can produce a sketch as complex and charming as the one on page 29 of *Boxen*.[2]

Most of the drawings in *Boxen*, however, are much less exciting. They are the stiff, laborious efforts of a child who understood perspective extremely early. They are skillful, clear, and detailed—but not delightful. One might get the impression that Lewis had a flash of artistic precocity when he was seven and that it immediately faded away.

By marvelous good fortune, however, the entire final page of "The King's Ring" is available just as the child Lewis penned it, but shrunk down to 2 by 3.5 inches. It does not appear in *Boxen*. It appears on page 98 of an earlier book, *C. S. Lewis: Images of His World* by Clyde S. Kilby and Douglas R. Gilbert (published by the William B. Eerdmans Company in 1973). With a magnifying glass, the page becomes fairly clear.

The page is numbered 24 in the upper left corner, and it contains the following:

> hath ~~clov~~ clove
> the earth in 2.[*]
> C U R T A I N
> THE END
> [*]the ancheint Mice belived
> that at sun-set the
> ~~the~~ sun cut a hole in
> the earth for its self.

The play ends with an illustration that was left out of the book *Boxen*. It shows Sir Peter Mouse and King Bunny posing triumphant over their prisoner, Hit—the mouse who stole the ring. King Bunny, alas, is a rumpled figure who didn't turn out right; he is probably supposed to be kneeling, and his elbows are prominent because his arms are very long. Hit is not much more than a stick figure with incredibly long arms. And charming Sir Peter is a tall skinny mouse in a tunic, like a lanky boy with the head of a mouse. Readers of *Boxen* are not told that Lewis ended his play with a picture that shows the thief being punished.

This final picture resembles in an immature way most of Lewis's art in *Boxen*, but it doesn't look like the four previous "King's Ring" illustrations at all. It makes one wonder if the child Lewis had help with the first four. Great help. If Warren Lewis had been allowed to publish *Boxen*, he might have told us truly that his mother or father drew the first four illustrations for their bright little playwright son, at his request.

"The Relief of Murry" (on pages 37-38 of *Boxen*) is closely related to "The King's Ring." In his preface to the 1982 book *On Stories and Other Essays on Literature*, [3] Hooper apparently described "The Relief of Murry" without naming it and said it is in the notebook that contains "To Mars and Back," elsewhere called Notebook III. That seems to be an error; Hooper later stated, in *Boxen*, that he found it in Notebook I with "The King's Ring." Furthermore, it looks as if the two illustrations for "The Relief of Murry," like the four mature illustrations for "The King's Ring," were done by a Lewis parent. First is a vigorous, fluid sketch of a dressed mouse with sword, and second is a troop of chivalrous mice in armor, one on a steed, all setting off to do battle. They are the work of a hastily careless but sure and talented hand. I think we have a precocious young child's story with adult sketches done at his request. (It should be remembered that C. S. Lewis was born with slightly abnormal hands and always lacked full digital dexterity.)

"To Mars and Back" presents a related problem.[4] In his preface to On Stories and Other Essays on Literature, Hooper not only placed it in the same notebook with "The Relief of Murry," but placed it in Lewis's early childhood, claiming that he wrote it when he was not much more than five or six years old. Actually, the first two pages of the story appear on page 104 of C. S. Lewis: Images of His World; readers can estimate the writer's age for themselves. But what readers have had no way to know until now is that Notebook III includes, along with "To Mars and Back," a story or diary entry in lofty style telling how eleven-year-old Lewis got up one bleak November morning at boarding school in 1909 and washed in icy dormitory water. I propose that "To Mars and Back" was written when Lewis was closer to age ten than age five, which would place the story after his mother's death. The most interesting aspect of these juvenilia details is the questions they raise about the dependability of the editing of all Lewis material.

Walter Hooper said on page 9 of his lengthy introduction that he regrets that not much of Lewis's earliest work survives, but that "all that has survived is in this book." That is odd, because there are five notebook pages of Lewis's earliest surviving work pictured on pages 98 and 99 of C. S. Lewis: Images of His World, and they are not included in Hooper's Boxen.

These five pages seem to be located in Hooper's Notebook I, with "The King's Ring." (These pages have rounded corners and 21 ruled lines, and the ratio of their dimensions is approximately 2 by 3.5.) On page 197 of *Boxen* we read that "The King's Ring" is in an account book with stiff black covers—the only one of its kind in the assorted Lewis juvenilia. (It seems to be the only one with rounded corners.) On page 9 of *Boxen* Hooper says his Notebook I contains "The King's Ring," "Manx against Manx," and "The Relief of Murry."

Clearly, the early material that is being left out of *Boxen* is relevant for anyone who wants to know all surviving details about Lewis's childhood. But the strange circumstances of the ownership and handling of the early childhood material present a literary mystery that is intriguing in its own right. Whether a detective story involves a missing ring or some missing juvenilia, the story can be fascinating by its very nature; but it does require patient accumulation of factual details. The juvenilia in *C. S. Lewis: Images of His World* has to be noted carefully for this reason.

First there is the important concluding illustration for "The King's Ring." Then there is on the facing page (page 25) a six-panel cartoon about a similar adventure. In the first panel a burglar mouse in a tunic, with long pipe-stem arms and legs, reaches into a large jar in the treasure room of a castle and says, "Dear me. O someone coming. I'll hide." In the second panel the burglar is down in the jar and says "Ah now I'm safe, hop they no one I'll will see Me."

In the third panel, a servant in a tunic picks up the large jar and says, "I have to take this off—." In the fourth panel the servant is stooping awkwardly on the edge of a bridge saying, "and as there is nothing in it throw it away!!" The jar has fallen into the water below, and a voice comes out saying "Oh!"

In the fifth panel the burglar can be seen inside the

jar under the water with fish swimming by; and he says, "Oh and I'm sinking." In the sixth panel the burglar, dead or alive, is being hoisted up onto the bridge with a long pole wielded by a mouse in an impressive uniform.

Warren Lewis was reportedly concerned that someone might steal away his hoard of juvenilia. It is interesting to imagine someone doing so and then discovering little C. S. Lewis's stern moral fable about burglary inside.

Another page pictured in Gilbert's book but left out of *Boxen* and not mentioned by Hooper in his supposedly exhaustive accounts is the conclusion of a description of some Animal-land geography. It tells that Murry was the capital of Mouse-land and Canon-town was the capital of Rabbit-land. Little Lewis's spelling is brave: "A twon is a large piece of land covered with buildings, most of wich tuch each other. The parts of a town bwetwen the houses are called streets or roads and are used for trafic to travel up and dwon. If a twon is verry small it is called a vilage. Vilgges are more prety than twons." This essay is followed by a banner that says "Fines" suspended between two funny little buildings with human legs (Lewis meant "Finis," The End).

Another page from Notebook I, reproduced on page 99 of *C. S. Lewis: Images of His World,* is devoted to some of the characters in "The King's Ring" in what appears to be an illustration for a similar story. Again a stiff boy-shaped mouse is the thief. It looks as if he is hiding in a large "oile" jar. Sir Big the frog and Mr. Icthyosaurus are sitting in the road, and a truly marvelous Sir Goose is about to disappear over the horizon. The words "Take any ruby" are written across the sky.

Because the book *Boxen* presents all kinds of minutiae concerning the Lewis juvenilia and is supposed to be complete, it seems peculiar that part of the material in Hooper's possession was not even mentioned, although it was in the same notebook as "The King's Ring." It has not been displayed, published, or described anywhere until now. For example, a page marked June 1907, shows a sketch of several people in a severe thunderstorm in a city, with a sign that says "Beware." On the facing page, marked "A Dream," a man with a cane is walking in the sky above a city and his top hat is falling off. On another page, five little men hunt sea creatures underwater, and on the facing page a large deep-sea diver poses in his gear with an ax in his hand. In the upper corner one man in a tunic beheads another with an ax. On another page a neatly diagrammed house features a trunk room and a servant's room in the attic.

Best of all, perhaps, is the page with a tidy, circular solar system which features "air" inside, "space" outside, and "unknown" under it all. The latter would make a wonderful illustration for the epilogue of C. S. Lewis's serious study *The Discarded Image*.[5] Hardly anyone has known that the design existed before its description here.

Although Walter Hooper says he obtained two childhood notebooks in 1963 from Lewis himself to help him with his Lewis research, the contents have never yet become available to other Lewis researchers. Even Lewis's chosen biographer Roger Lancelyn Green never got to see the originals or photocopies of them. An entire generation of students of C. S. Lewis are aging and gradually dying away without ever getting to examine photocopies of Hooper's Lewis material (most of it rescued from the Lewis bonfire) when doing research in the Marion E. Wade Center or the Bodleian Library.[6]

All is fair in love and scholarship, perhaps. Some

specialists are eager to disseminate research materials in their own fields, as Lewis would have done, and others consider such disinterested commitment to public knowledge as naive. In the ordinary course of affairs, there is no professional obligation for scholars to pass on their advantages to others who might become competitors. But in this particular case, the circumstances are extraordinary and call for explanation.

In June 1972, professional photographer Douglas R. Gilbert visited Oxford and took many pictures of the Major's memorabilia, some of which would appear in *C. S. Lewis: Images of His World* one year later. Gilbert says that he laid out books, notebooks, and papers on the rug of the Kilns and photographed them there. He keeps all his photography projects. His photographs include several from the earliest Lewis juvenilia, property of Warren Lewis in 1972. Gilbert has pictures of pages in the "The King's Ring" notebook (I) and the "Geography of Animal-land" notebook (III).

Two months after the photography session, in August, Warren Lewis went to Ireland for a visit. He did not feel well in 1972, having had a pacemaker installed in January. In Ireland his health worsened, and he had to stay there all winter. During that period Leonard and Mollie Miller took care of the Kilns and the Major's business, and Leonard Miller flew to Ireland and visited Warren Lewis there for several days every month.[7] Early in April 1973, Warren Lewis returned to Oxford; he died at the Kilns a few days later, on April 9. So it was that less than one year after American Douglas Gilbert went to the Kilns to photograph Warren Lewis's personal collection, the collection was sent to Illinois. Gilbert could have waited and photographed it there.

But Gilbert would have lost some of his photographs if he had waited, because the two early notebooks containing "The King's Ring" and "Geography of Animal-land" never went to Illinois. Hooper announced years later that they had been his since 1963, seemingly oblivious to the fact that Gilbert had handled them and photographed them in the Kilns in 1972. Gilbert sincerely believed they were the Major's property. Although it is possible that there is a simple explanation for the contradiction, the obvious discrepancy has never been acknowledged or explained in the fifteen years since it arose. The silence itself is disturbing.

Although Gilbert published photographs of some of this material in his book in 1973, Walter Hooper gave the impression in Boxen in 1985 that he had been guarding the material in his private collection for over twenty years, and that it was now appearing for the first time. Relatively few people now recall Gilbert's inclusion of some early juvenilia.

Boxen's introduction is long and enthusiastic, but the cumulative effect of the writing style is confusing. For example, Hooper says that the little stories "Manx against Manx" and "The Relief of Murry" form a transition between the modern setting of "The King's Ring" and a medieval setting. This seems to be a slip of the pen, because "The King's Ring" is itself medieval.

"Honored as I am in being appointed to edit the stories, I suppose my old friend would, with his usual gaiety, call me that future Boxonologist. He might even have suggested me as the first holder of the Lord Big Chair of Boxonology." So Hooper spoke of himself in his glowing introduction to Boxen. He told how much he enjoyed reading the juvenilia while he lived with C. S. Lewis in

1963. He said that Lewis talked with him about it at some length.

At this point in the introduction Hooper gave a startling interpretation to a well-known statement by the child Lewis. In his diary Lewis had described himself briefly and had included the fact that he had a bad temper like his father. Hooper claimed in *Boxen*, "When Jack spoke of himself . . . as having his father's 'bad temper' he almost certainly meant that he shared his father's gift for oratory."[8] A peculiar idea.

At any rate, some of the needless confusion in *Boxen* can be sorted out. In addition to the materials in it from the Wade Center ("Boxen," "The Locked Door and Thankyu," and "The Sailor") and an essay contributed by Hugh Cecil ("History of Animal-land," location not mentioned), *Boxen* contains the following:

1. From Notebook I, which C. S. Lewis gave to Walter Hooper in the summer of 1963: "The King's Ring," "Manx against Manx," and "The Relief of Murry."

2. From Notebook II, which Walter Hooper saved from the Lewis bonfire: "History of Mouseland from Stone-Age to Bublish," "The Chess Monograph, Part I," "Life of Little Mr. White" (page 11), and "How To Make Men Picturesc" (pages 15 and 16).

3. From Notebook III, which C. S. Lewis gave to Walter Hooper in the summer of 1963: "The Chess Monograph, Part II," and "The Geography of Animal-land."

4. From a certain exercise book which Walter Hooper saved from the Lewis bonfire: "Encyclopedia Boxoniana."

This last material is what the adult C. S. Lewis wrote in September 1927 and April 1928, while visiting his father at the family home. Unfortunately, although "Encyclopedia Boxoniana" is meant both fondly and playfully, it is both dull and long-winded. Parts of it do not sound at all like C. S. Lewis. (Would the adult Lewis intrusively refer to one king's ring as "the crown jewels of Animalland?")

The mock-scholarly tone appropriate for satirizing poor English is not used with that particular purpose in "Encyclopedia Boxoniana," and so readers are left wondering why Lewis wrote dreadful sentences such as this: "As regards the configuration of the principle [sic] land masses all the extant maps show a remarkable uniformity, but as regards the scale it is quite impossible to reconcile any of the maps with the distances implied in the texts where journies [sic] are described."[9] Readers are supposed to believe that one of the greatest masters of English in our century wrote this when he was already teaching at Oxford. I don't think he could have written such prose unless he had been delirious with fever.

Lewis is not satirizing his own Boxen materials, and he is not satirizing pompous scholarship, and so the following sentence appears inexplicable: "To draw out all that can be deduced from the texts, to attempt the solution of all problems and the removal of all contradictions in the light of general probability and skilful hypothesis, would have been to anticipate the future Boxonologist rather than to provide him with his tools."[10] Really.

And for content as well as style, this grandiose declaration about his childhood creations may be the most unLewisian sentence of all: "And this is a matter of absorbing interest; to trace the process by which an attic full of commonplace childrens' [sic] toys became a world as consistent and self-sufficient as that of the Iliad or the Barsetshire novels, would be no small contribution to general psychology."[11] Neither the words, the attitude, nor the wrong punctuation of children's are true C. S. Lewis, some readers suspect.

A sprinkling of spelling errors in the text might make it look more authentic to readers who know that Lewis was an imperfect speller. But to others it looks like a ploy.

Questioning the validity of "Encyclopedia Boxoniana," which C. S. Lewis supposedly wrote as a mature man, is not to doubt his fondness for his childhood creations. But for some readers, the most interesting part of *Boxen* is "The King's Ring," and from there on the book becomes less and less interesting. "Encyclopedia Boxoniana," at the end, whether by Lewis or not, is almost unendurable.

Roger Lancelyn Green, who had discussed Lewis's juvenilia with him and who saw how precocious it was, nevertheless admitted frankly in the biography that as literature Boxen was "intensely dull."[12] Dr. Clyde S. Kilby was delighted to place much of the juvenilia in the Marion E. Wade Center, but he felt that it was so dull it shouldn't be published. If published, he reasoned, it would surely sell because of the name of its author; but it would bore the purchasers. (He had not seen the most boring part, "Encyclopedia Boxoniana.") History seems to be bearing out Kilby's prediction.

The review commending *Boxen* in the October 1986 issue of *Eternity* magazine[13] gave the impression that the reviewer had not forced himself to look at the first section of the book, much less to read it. He said that the first section consisted of a group of short plays (it consisted of one short play and various brief historical accounts), and that it was apparently written when Lewis was in elementary school (he did not attend elementary school, as the introduction makes clear).

For the bulk of the book, the reviewer remarked, "These writings are obviously from the pre-Christian Lewis and reflect his classically romantic mind." That idea seems to reflect an extremely sleepy mind. But inflated or overly-innocent reviews of this book will do the world little harm.

Frankly, even possible additions or omissions in *Boxen* itself are of minimal significance to the reading public. The only two people who cared ardently about the Boxen material are long buried together under a common marker in the Headington churchyard.

Since *Boxen* is of little interest to most readers, what difference does it make whether it is handled scrupulously or not? An answer can be found in "The King's Ring" itself.

Near the end of "The King's Ring," helpful Sir Goose asked Sir Peter Mouse and Sir Big why all this fuss was made about the missing ring when King Bunny could have got a new ring which would have been just as good.

And they answered, "Ah, but this ring was an airloom."

That suggests the real reason why some of us are exclaiming like Sir Peter, "Who!! Which!! Where!! When!! Why!! What!! How!!"

When asked "Why all this fuss about what is or isn't correct and genuine in the posthumous C. S. Lewis books, and what difference does it make?" we can echo Sir Peter: "Ah but this was an *air-loom* to us." We count Lewis and whatever he created as part of our heritage.

Appendix 1, Notes
1. Roger Lancelyn Green and Walter Hooper, C. S. *Lewis: A Biography* (London: Collins, 1974), 28.
2. The third "King's Ring" illustration includes all of these: Mr. Icthus-oress sitting on a bench with his harp nearby; the wonderful Golliwog next to him with a staff; the mouse Bob in his monk's habit; the mouse Tom behind him with his spinning wheel nearby; playing cards that have fallen on the floor; a barred window; a lighted wall sconce; and a table with a glowing candle on it.
3. C. S. Lewis, *On Stories and Other Essays on Literature* (New York: Harcourt Brace Jovanovich, 1982), x.

4. There is no way to know yet how long "To Mars and Back" is. It begins with a narrator named Bensin invited to go to Mars in a "vessel" with a chum of his. He has a "mild intrest" in astronomy, but is doubtful about the trip. He decides to go to Southampton and perhaps from there to central Africa and Mars. This is all on the first two pages.

5. C. S. Lewis, *The Discarded Image* (Cambridge: University Press, 1964), 216-23.

6. Douglas R. Gilbert's private photography file provides tantalizing glimpses into the Lewis juvenilia that did not find its way to the Marion E. Wade Center. His pictures of Notebook III material include, in addition to the beginning of "To Mars and Back" and the dormitory scene, a page from an illustrated story about Mr. Bull and a red-haired Indian in shiny boots who came in and shook snow on the Turkey carpet. The existence of this story has never been mentioned to the public until now.

   One can assume that Gilbert wishes he had photographed much more of Notebooks I and III while they were in his hands in The Kilns. Surely students of Lewis's early life wish he had done so.

7. Leonard Miller described this period and what he saw as chronic mismanagement of the business affairs of the Lewis brothers in the tape recording made at the Miller home in Eynsham, England, on 27 December 1975.

8. C. S. Lewis, *Boxen* (San Diego: Harcourt Brace Jovanovich, 1985), 17.

9. Ibid., 206.

10. Ibid., 196.

11. Ibid., 197.

12. Green and Hooper, *C. S. Lewis*, 23.

13. Philip G. Houghton, "C. S. Lewis's *Boxen*," *Eternity*, October 1986, 55-56. Houghton observes, "Lewis fans will welcome this book with open arms. Many have been waiting for decades to learn more of Boxen."

Appendix 2

LET'S WASH OUT ALL THE WISH BUSINESS

These are the three Lewis letters Sheldon Vanauken made public property:

14/12/50

Dear Mr. Vanauken,

My own position at the threshold of Xianity was exactly the opposite of yours. You wish it were true; I strongly hoped it was *not*. At least, that was my conscious wish: you may suspect that I had unconscious wishes of quite a different sort and that it was these which finally shoved me in. True: but then I may equally suspect that under your conscious wish that it were true, there lurks a strong unconscious wish that it were not. What this works out to is that all the modern thinking, however useful it may be for explaining the origin of an error which you already know to be an error, is perfectly useless in deciding which of two beliefs is the error and which is the truth. For (a.) One never knows all one's wishes, and (b.) In very big questions, such as this, even one's conscious wishes are nearly always engaged on both sides. What I think one can say with certainty is this: the notion that everyone *would like* Xianity to be true, and that therefore all atheists are brave men who have accepted the defeat of all their deepest desires, is simply impudent nonsense. Do you think people like Stalin, Hitler, Haldane, Stapledon (a corking good writer, by the way) wd. be pleased on waking up one morning to find that they were not their own masters, that they had a Master and a Judge, that there was nothing even in the deepest recesses of their thoughts about which they cd. say to Him 'Keep out! Private. This is *my* business'? Do you? *Rats!* Their first reaction wd. be (as mine was) rage and terror. And I v. much doubt whether even you wd. find it *simply* pleasant. Isn't the truth this: that it wd. gratify some of our desires (ones we feel in fact pretty seldom) and outrage a good many others? So let's wash out all the wish business. It never helped anyone to solve any problem yet.

I don't agree with your picture of the history of religion—Christ, Buddha, Mohammed and others elaborating on an original simplicity. I believe Buddhism to be a simplification of Hinduism and Islam to be a simplification of Xianity. Clear, lucid, transparent, simple religion (Tao *plus* a shadowy, ethical god in the background) is a late development, usually arising among highly educated people in great cities. What you really start with in ritual, myth, and mystery, the death & return of Balder or Osiris, the dances, the initiations, the sacrifices, the divine kings. Over against that are the Philosophers, Aristotle or Confucius, hardly religion at all. The only two systems in which the mysteries and the philosophies come together are Hinduism & Xianity: there you get both the Metaphysics and Cult (continuous with primeval cults). That is why my first step was to be sure that one or the other of these had the answer. For the reality can't be one that appeals either only to savages *or* only to high brows. Real things aren't like that (e.g. *matter* is the first most obvious thing you meet—milk, chocolates, apples, and also the object of quantum physics). There is no question of just a crowd of disconnected religions. The choice is between (a.) The materialist world picture: wh. I can't believe. (b.) The real archaic primitive religions; wh. are not moral enough. (c.) The (claimed) fulfillment of these in Hinduism. (d.) The claimed fulfillment of these in Xianity. But the weakness of Hinduism is that it *doesn't* really merge the two strands. Unredeemable savage religion goes on in the village; the Hermit philosophizes in the forest: and neither really interfaces with the other. It is only Xianity which compels a high brow like me to partake of a ritual blood feast, and also compels a central African convert to attempt an enlightened code of ethics.

Have you ever tried Chesterton's *The Everlasting Man?* The best popular apologetic I know.

Meanwhile, the attempt to practice *Tao* is certainly the right line. Have you read the *Analects* of Confucius? He ends up by saying, 'This is the Tao. I do not know if anyone has ever kept it.' That's significant: one can really go direct from there to the Epistle of the Romans.

I don't know if any of this is the least use. Be sure to write again, or call, if you think I can be of any help.

Yours sincerely
C. S. Lewis

23 Dec. 1950
Dear Mr. Vanauken

The contradiction 'we must have faith to believe and must believe to have faith' belongs to the same class as those by which the Eleatic philosophers proved that all motion is impossible. And there are many others. You can't swim unless you can support yourself in water & you can't support yourself in water unless you can swim.

Or again, in an act of volition (e.g. getting up in the morning) is the very beginning of the act itself voluntary or involuntary? If voluntary then you must have willed it, . . you were willing it already, . . it was not really the beginning. If involuntary, then the continuation of the act (being determined by the first movement) is involuntary too. But in spite of this we *do* swim, & we *do* get out of bed.

I do not think there is a *demonstrative* proof (like Euclid) of Christianity, nor of the existence of matter, nor of the good will & honesty of my best & oldest friends. I think all three (except perhaps the second) far more probable than the alternatives. The case for Xianity in general is well given by Chesterton; and I tried to do something in my *Broadcast Talks*. As to *why* God doesn't make it demonstratively clear; are we sure that He is even interested in the kind of Theism which wd. be a compelled logical assent to a conclusive argument? Are *we* interested in it in personal matters? I demand from my friend a trust in my good faith which is *certain* without demonstrative proof. It wouldn't be confidence at all if he waited for rigorous proof. Hang it all, the very fairy tales embody the truth. Othello believed in Desdemona's innocence when it was proved: but that was too late. 'His praise is lost who stays till all commend.' The magnanimity, the generosity which will trust on a reasonable probability, is required of us. But supposing one believed and was wrong after all? Why, then you wd. have paid the universe a compliment it doesn't deserve. Your error wd. even so be more interesting & important than the reality. And yet how cd. that be? How cd. an idiotic universe have produced creatures whose mere dreams are so much stronger, better, subtler than itself?

Note that life after death which still seems to you the essential thing, was itself a *late* revelation. God trained the Hebrews for centuries to believe in Him without promising them an afterlife, and, blessings on Him, he trained me in the same way for about a year. It is like the disguised prince in a fairy tale who wins the heroine's love *before* she knows he is anything more than a wood-cutter. What wd. be a bribe if it came first had better come last.

It is quite clear from what you say that you have *conscious* wishes on both sides. And now, another point about *wishes*. A wish may lead to false beliefs, granted. But what does the existence of the wish suggest? At one time I was much impressed by Arnold's line 'Nor does the being hungry prove that we have bread.' But surely tho' it doesn't prove that one particular man will *get* food, it *does* prove that there is such a thing as food! i.e. if we were a species that didn't normally eat, weren't designed to eat, wd. we feel hungry? You say the materialist universe is 'ugly.' I wonder how you discovered that! If you are really a product of a materialistic universe, how is it you don't feel at home there? Do fish complain of the sea for being wet? Or if they did, would that fact itself not strongly suggest that they had not always been, or wd. not always be, purely aquatic creatures? Notice how we are perpetually *surprised* at Time. ('How time flies! Fancy John being grown-up and married! I can hardly believe it!') In heaven's name, why? Unless, indeed, there is something about us that is *not* temporal.

Total humility is not in the Tao because the Tao (as such) says nothing about the Object to which it wd. be the right response: just as there is no law about railways in the acts of Q. Elizabeth. But from the degree of respect wh. the Tao demands for ancestors, parents, elders, & teachers, it is quite clear what the Tao *wd.* prescribe towards an object such as God.

But I think you are already in the meshes of the net! The Holy Spirit is after you. I doubt if you'll get away!

Yours,
C. S. Lewis

17/4/51

Dear Vanauken

My prayers are answered. No: a glimpse is not a vision. But to a man on a mountain road by night, a glimpse of the next three feet of road may matter more than a vision of the horizon. And there must perhaps be always just enough lack of demonstrative certainty to make free choice possible: for what could we do but accept if the faith were like the multiplication table?

There will be a counter attack on you, you know, so don't be too alarmed when it comes.

The enemy will not see you vanish into God's company without an effort to reclaim you.

Be busy learning to pray and (if you have made up yr. mind on the denominational question) get confirmed.

Blessings on you and a hundred thousand welcomes. Make use of me in any way you please: and let us pray for each other always.

Yours,
C. S. Lewis

INDEX

171